C. S. LEWIS

A GRIEF OBSERVED

"For this is one of the miracles of love; it gives—
to both, but perhaps especially to the woman
—a power of seeing through its own enchant-
ment and yet not being disenchanted."

"The author has done something I had believed
impossible—assuaged his own grief by convey-
ing it . . ."

—Anne Freemantle

"Destined to be a profound comfort to many
thousands and may well take its place among
the great devotional books of the age."

—Chad Walsh

C. S. LEWIS

A GRIEF OBSERVED

Afterword by Chad Walsh

BANTAM BOOKS
TORONTO · NEW YORK · LONDON · SYDNEY · AUCKLAND

A GRIEF OBSERVED

*A Bantam Book / published by arrangement with
The Seabury Press, Inc.*

PRINTING HISTORY

First published in England by Faber and Faber Limited

Seabury Press edition published February 1963

2nd printing . . . . . . January 1964	6th printing . . . . April 1970
3rd printing . . . . . February 1965	7th printing . . . . April 1972
4th printing . . . . July 1966	8th printing . . . . November 1973
5th printing . . . . June 1967	9th printing . . . . April 1974

Bantam edition / March 1976

2nd printing . . . . December 1976	5th printing . . . . July 1979
3rd printing . . . . . December 1977	6th printing . . . . March 1980
4th printing . . . . October 1978	7th printing . . . . . December 1980

ISBN 0-553-14840-0

Published simultaneously in the United States and Canada

Bantam Books are published by Bantam Books, Inc. Its trademark, consisting of the words "Bantam Books" and the por-
trayal of a bantam, is Registered in U.S. Patent and Trademark
Office and in other countries. Marca Registrada. Bantam
Books, Inc., 666 Fifth Avenue, New York, New York 10103.

PRINTED IN THE UNITED STATES OF AMERICA

16 15 14 13

A GRIEF OBSERVED

I

No one ever told me that grief felt so like fear. I am not afraid, but the sensation is like being afraid. The same fluttering in the stomach, the same restlessness, the yawning. I keep on swallowing.

At other times it feels like being mildly drunk, or concussed. There is a sort of invisible blanket between the world and me. I find it hard to take in what anyone says. Or perhaps, hard to want to take it in. It is so uninteresting. Yet I want the others to be about me. I dread the moments when the house is empty. If only they would talk to one another and not to me.

There are moments, most unexpectedly, when something inside me tries to assure me that I don't really mind so much, not so very much, after all. Love is not the whole of a man's life. I was happy before I ever met H. I've plenty of what are called "resources." People get over these things. Come, I shan't do so badly. One is ashamed to listen to this voice but it seems for a little to be making out a good case. Then comes a sudden jab of red-hot memory and all this "common-sense" vanishes like an ant in the mouth of a furnace.

On the rebound one passes into tears and pathos. Maudlin tears. I almost prefer the moments of agony. These are at least clean and honest. But the bath of self-pity, the wallow, the loathsome sticky-sweet pleasure of indulging it—that disgusts me. And even while I'm doing it I know it leads me to misrepresent H. herself. Give that mood its head and in a few minutes I shall have substituted for the real woman a mere doll to be blubbered over. Thank God the memory of her is still too strong (will it always be too strong?) to let me get away with it.

For H. wasn't like that at all. Her mind was lithe and quick and muscular as a leopard. Passion, tenderness and pain were all equally unable to disarm it. It scented the first whiff of cant or slush; then sprang, and knocked you over before you knew what was happening. How many bubbles of mine she pricked! I soon learned not to talk rot to her unless I did it for the sheer plea‚ sure—and there's another red‚hot jab—of being exposed and laughed at. I was never less silly than as H.'s lover.

And no one ever told me about the laziness of grief. Except at my job—where the ma‚ chine seems to run on much as usual—I loathe the slightest effort. Not only writing but even reading a letter is too much. Even shaving. What does it matter now whether my cheek is rough or smooth? They say an unhappy man wants distractions—something to take him out of himself. Only as a dog-tired man wants an extra blanket on a cold night; he'd rather lie there shivering than get up and find one. It's easy to see why the lonely become untidy; finally, dirty and disgusting.

Meanwhile, where is God? This is one of the most disquieting symptoms. When you are happy, so happy that you have no sense of needing Him, so happy that you are tempted to feel His claims upon you as an interruption, if you remember yourself and turn to Him with gratitude and praise, you will be—or so it feels—welcomed with open arms. But go to Him when your need is desperate, when all other help is vain, and what do you find? A door slammed in your face, and a sound of bolting and double bolting on the inside. After that, silence. You may as well turn away. The longer you wait, the more emphatic the silence will become. There are no lights in the windows. It might be an empty house. Was it ever inhabited? It seemed so once. And that seeming was as strong as this. What can this mean? Why is He so present a commander in our time of prosperity and so very absent a help in time of trouble?

I tried to put some of these thoughts to C. this afternoon. He reminded me that the same thing seems to have happened to Christ: "Why hast thou forsaken me?" I know. Does that make it easier to understand?

Not that I am (I think) in much danger of ceasing to believe in God. The real danger is of coming to believe such dreadful things about Him. The conclusion I dread is not, "So there's no God after all," but, "So this is what God's really like. Deceive yourself no longer."

Our elders submitted and said, "Thy will be done." How often had bitter resentment been stifled through sheer terror and an act of love—yes, in every sense, an act—put on to hide the operation?

Of course it's easy enough to say that God seems absent at our greatest need because He *is* absent—non-existent. But then why does He seem so present when, to put it quite frankly, we don't ask for Him?

One thing, however, marriage has done for me. I can never again believe that religion is manufactured out of our unconscious, starved desires and is a substitute for sex. For those few years H. and I feasted on love; every mode of it—solemn and merry, romantic and realistic, sometimes as dramatic as a thunderstorm, sometimes as comfortable and unemphatic as putting on your soft slippers. No cranny of heart or body remained unsatisfied. If God were a substitute for love we ought to have lost all interest in Him. Who'd bother about substitutes when he has the thing itself? But that isn't what happens. We both knew we wanted something besides one another—quite a different kind of something, a quite different kind of want. You might as well say that when lovers have one another they will never want to read, or eat—or breathe.

After the death of a friend, years ago, I had for some time a most vivid feeling of certainty about his continued life; even his enhanced life. I have begged to be given even one hundredth part of the same assurance about H. There is no answer. Only the locked door, the iron curtain, the vacuum, absolute zero. "Them as asks don't get." I was a fool to ask. For now, even if that assurance came I should distrust it. I should think it a self-hypnosis induced by my own prayers.

At any rate I must keep clear of the spiritualists. I promised H. I would. She knew
something of those circles.

Keeping promises to the dead, or to anyone
else, is very well. But I begin to see that "respect for the wishes of the dead" is a trap.
Yesterday I stopped myself only in time
from saying about some trifle, "H. wouldn't
have liked that." This is unfair to the others.
I should soon be using "what H. would
have liked" as an instrument of domestic
tyranny; with her supposed likings becoming a thinner and thinner disguise for my
own.

I cannot talk to the children about her. The
moment I try, there appears on their faces
neither grief, nor love, nor fear, nor pity, but
the most fatal of all non-conductors, embarrassment. They look as if I were committing
an indecency. They are longing for me to
stop. I felt just the same after my own

mother's death when my father mentioned her. I can't blame them. It's the way boys are.

I sometimes think that shame, mere awk-ward, senseless shame, does as much towards preventing good acts and straightforward happiness as any of our vices can do. And not only in boyhood.

Or are the boys right? What would H. her-self think of this terrible little notebook to which I come back and back? Are these jottings morbid? I once read the sentence "I lay awake all night with toothache, thinking about toothache and about lying awake." That's true to life. Part of every misery is, so to speak, the misery's shadow or reflection: the fact that you don't merely suffer but have to keep on thinking about the fact that you suffer. I not only live each endless day in grief, but live each day thinking about liv-ing each day in grief. Do these notes merely aggravate that side of it? Merely confirm the monotonous, tread-mill march of the mind round one subject? But what am I to do? I must have some drug, and reading isn't a strong enough drug now. By writing it all down (all?—no: one thought in a hundred) I believe I get a little outside it. That's how I'd defend it to H. But ten to one she'd see a hole in the defense.

It isn't only the boys either. An odd by-product of my loss is that I'm aware of being an embarrassment to everyone I meet. At work, at the club, in the street, I see people, as they approach me, trying to make up their minds whether they'll "say something about it" or not. I hate it if they do, and if they don't. Some funk it altogether. R. has been avoiding me for a week. I like best the well-brought-up young men, almost boys, who walk up to me as if I were a dentist, turn very red, get it over, and then edge away to the bar as quickly as they decently can. Perhaps the bereaved ought to be isolated in special settlements like lepers.

To some I'm worse than an embarrassment. I am a death's head. Whenever I meet a happily married pair I can feel them both thinking, "One or other of us must some day be as he is now."

At first I was very afraid of going to places where H. and I had been happy—our favorite pub, our favorite wood. But I decided to do it at once—like sending a pilot up again as soon as possible after he's had a crash. Unexpectedly, it makes no difference. Her absence is no more emphatic in those places than anywhere else. It's not local at all. I suppose that if one were forbidden all salt one wouldn't notice it much more in any one food than in another. Eating in general would be different, every day, at every meal. It is like that. The act of living is different all through. Her absence is like the sky, spread over everything.

But no, that is not quite accurate. There is one place where her absence comes locally home to me, and it is a place I can't avoid. I mean my own body. It had such a different importance while it was the body of H.'s lover. Now it's like an empty house. But don't let me deceive myself. This body would become important to me again, and pretty quickly, if I thought there was anything wrong with it.

Cancer, and cancer, and cancer. My mother, my father, my wife. I wonder who is next in the queue.

Yet H. herself, dying of it, and well knowing the fact, said that she had lost a great deal of her old horror at it. When the reality came, the name and the idea were in some degree disarmed. And up to a point I very nearly understood. This is important. One never meets just Cancer, or War, or Unhappiness (or Happiness). One only meets each hour or moment that comes. All manner of ups and downs. Many bad spots in our best times, many good ones in our worst. One never gets the total impact of what we call "the thing itself." But we call it wrongly. The thing itself is simply all these ups and downs: the rest is a name or an idea.

It is incredible how much happiness, even how much gaiety, we sometimes had together after all hope was gone. How long, how tranquilly, how nourishingly, we talked together that last night!

And yet, not quite together. There's a limit to the "one flesh." You can't really share someone else's weakness, or fear or pain. What you feel may be bad. It might conceivably be as bad as what the other felt, though I should distrust anyone who claimed that it was. But it would still be quite different. When I speak of fear, I mean the merely animal fear, the recoil of the organism from its destruction; the smothery feeling; the sense of being a rat in a trap. It can't be transferred. The mind can sympathize; the body, less. In one way the bodies of lovers can do it least. All their love passages have trained them to have, not identical, but complementary, correlative, even opposite, feelings about one another.

We both knew this. I had my miseries, not hers; she had hers, not mine. The end of hers would be the coming of age of mine. We were setting out on different roads. This cold truth, this terrible traffic regulation ("You, Madam, to the right—you, Sir, to the left") is just the beginning of the separation which is death itself.

And this separation, I suppose, waits for all. I have been thinking of H. and myself as peculiarly unfortunate in being torn apart. But presumably all lovers are. She once said to me, "Even if we both died at exactly the same moment, as we lie here side by side, it would be just as much a separa‑tion as the one you're so afraid of." Of course she didn't *know*, any more than I do. But she was near death; near enough to make a good shot. She used to quote, "Alone into the Alone." She said it felt like that. And how immensely improbable that it should be otherwise! Time and space and body were the very things that brought us together; the telephone wires by which we communicated. Cut one off, or cut both off simultaneously. Either way, mustn't the conversation stop?

Unless you assume that some other means of communication—utterly different, yet do‑ing the same work, would be immediately substituted. But then, what conceivable point could there be in severing the old ones? Is God a clown who whips away your bowl of soup one moment in order, next moment, to replace it with another bowl of the same soup? Even nature isn't such a clown as that. She never plays exactly the same tune twice.

It is hard to have patience with people who say, "There is no death," or, "Death doesn't matter." There is death. And whatever is matters. And whatever happens has consequences, and it and they are irrevocable and irreversible. You might as well say that birth doesn't matter. I look up at the night sky. Is anything more certain than that in all those vast times and spaces, if I were allowed to search them, I should nowhere find her face, her voice, her touch? She died. She is dead. Is the word so difficult to learn?

I have no photograph of her that's any good. I cannot even see her face distinctly in my imagination. Yet the odd face of some stranger seen in a crowd this morning may come before me in vivid perfection the moment I close my eyes tonight. No doubt, the explanation is simple enough. We have seen the faces of those we know best so variously, from so many angles, in so many lights, with so many expressions—waking, sleeping, laughing, crying, eating, talking, thinking—that all the impressions crowd into our memory together and cancel out into a mere blur. But her voice is still vivid. The remembered voice—that can turn me at any moment to a whimpering child.

II

FOR the first time I have looked back and read these notes. They appall me. From the way I've been talking anyone would think that H.'s death mattered chiefly for its effect on myself. Her point of view seems to have dropped out of sight. Have I forgotten the moment of bitterness when she cried out, "And there was so much to live for"? Happiness had not come to her early in life. A thousand years of it would not have made her *blasée*. Her palate for all the joys of sense and intellect and spirit was fresh and unspoiled. Nothing would have been wasted on her. She liked more things and liked them more than anyone I have known. A noble hunger, long unsatisfied, met at last its proper food, and almost instantly the food was snatched away. Fate (or whatever it is) delights to produce a great capacity and then frustrate it. Beethoven went deaf. By our standards a mean joke; the monkey trick of a spiteful imbecile.

I must think more about H. and less about myself.

Yes, that sounds very well. But there's a snag. I am thinking about her nearly always. Thinking of the H. facts—real words, looks, laughs, and actions of hers. But it is my own mind that selects and groups them. Already, less than a month after her death, I can feel the slow, insidious beginning of a process that will make the H. I think of into a more and more imaginary woman. Founded on fact, no doubt. I shall put in nothing fictitious (or I hope I shan't). But won't the composition inevitably become more and more my own? The reality is no longer there to check me, to pull me up short, as the real H. so often did, so unexpectedly, by being so thoroughly herself and not me.

The most precious gift that marriage gave me was this constant impact of something very close and intimate yet all the time unmistakably other, resistant—in a word, real. Is all that work to be undone? Is what I shall still call H. to sink back horribly into being not much more than one of my old bachelor pipe-dreams? Oh my dear, my dear, come back for one moment and drive that miserable phantom away. Oh God, God, why did you take such trouble to force this creature out of its shell if it is now doomed to crawl back—to be sucked back —into it?

Today I had to meet a man I haven't seen for ten years. And all that time I had thought I was remembering him well—how he looked and spoke and the sort of things he said. The first five minutes of the real man shattered the image completely. Not that he had changed. On the contrary. I kept on thinking, "Yes, of course, of course. I'd forgotten that he thought that—or disliked this, or knew so-and-so—or jerked his head back that way." I had known all these things once and I recognized them the moment I met them again. But they had all faded out of my mental picture of him, and when they were all replaced by his actual presence the total effect was quite astonishingly different from the image I had carried about with me for those ten years. How can I hope that this will not happen to my memory of H.? That it is not happening already? Slowly, quietly, like snow-flakes—like the small flakes that come when it is going to snow all night—little flakes of me, my impressions, my selections, are settling down on the image of her. The real shape will be quite hidden in the end. Ten minutes—ten seconds—of the real H. would correct all this. And yet, even if those ten seconds were allowed me, one second later the little flakes would begin to fall again. The rough, sharp, cleansing tang of her otherness is gone.

What pitiable cant to say, "She will live forever in my memory!" *Live?* That is exactly what she won't do. You might as well think like the old Egyptians that you can keep the dead by embalming them. Will nothing persuade us that they are gone? What's left? A corpse, a memory, and (in some versions) a ghost. All mockeries or horrors. Three more ways of spelling the word *dead*. It was H. I loved. As if I wanted to fall in love with my memory of her, an image in my own mind! It would be a sort of incest.

I remember being rather horrified one summer morning long ago when a burly, cheerful laboring man, carrying a hoe and a watering pot came into our churchyard and, as he pulled the gate behind him, shouted over his shoulder to two friends, "See you later, I'm just going to visit Mum." He meant he was going to weed and water and generally tidy up her grave. It horrified me because this mode of sentiment, all this churchyard stuff, was and is simply hateful, even inconceivable, to me. But in the light of my recent thoughts I am beginning to wonder whether, if one could take that man's line (I can't), there isn't a good deal to be said for it. A six-by-three-foot flower-bed had become Mum. That was his symbol for her, his link with her. Caring for it was visiting her. May this not be in one way better than preserving and caressing an image in one's own memory? The grave and the image are equally links with the irrecoverable and symbols for the unimaginable. But the image has the added disadvantage that it will do whatever you want. It will smile or frown, be tender, gay, ribald, or argumentative just as your mood demands. It is a puppet of which you hold the strings. Not yet of course. The reality is still too fresh; genuine and wholly involuntary memories can still, thank God, at any moment rush in and tear the strings out of my hands. But the fatal obedience of the image, its insipid dependence on me, is bound to increase. The flower-bed on the other hand is an obstinate, resistant, often intractable bit of reality, just as Mum in her lifetime doubtless was. As H. was.

Or as H. is. Can I honestly say that I believe she now is anything? The vast majority of the people I meet, say, at work, would certainly think she is not. Though naturally they wouldn't press the point on me. Not just now anyway. What do I really think? I have always been able to pray for the other dead, and I still do, with some confidence. But when I try to pray for H., I halt. Bewilderment and amazement come over me. I have a ghastly sense of unreality, of speaking into a vacuum about a nonentity.

The reason for the difference is only too plain. You never know how much you really believe anything until its truth or falsehood becomes a matter of life and death to you. It is easy to say you believe a rope to be strong and sound as long as you are merely using it to cord a box. But suppose you had to hang by that rope over a precipice. Wouldn't you then first discover how much you really trusted it? The same with people. For years I would have said that I had perfect confidence in B.R. Then came the moment when I had to decide whether I would or would not trust him with a really important secret. That threw quite a new light on what I called my "confidence" in him. I discovered that there was no such thing. Only a real risk tests the reality of a belief. Apparently the faith—I thought it faith—which enables me to pray for the other dead has seemed strong only because I have never really cared, not desperately, whether they existed or not. Yet I thought I did.

But there are other difficulties. "Where is she now?" That is, *in what place* is she *at the present time*. But if H. is not a body—and the body I loved is certainly no longer she—she is in no place at all. And "the present time" is a date or point in our time series. It is as if she were on a journey without me and I said, looking at my watch, "I wonder is she at Euston now." But unless she is proceeding at sixty seconds a minute along this same timeline that all we living people travel by, what does *now* mean? If the dead are not in time, or not in our sort of time, is there any clear difference, when we speak of them, between *was* and *is* and *will be*?

Kind people have said to me, "She is with God." In one sense that is most certain. She is, like God, incomprehensible and unimaginable.

But I find that this question, however important it may be in itself, is not after all very important in relation to grief. Suppose that the earthly lives she and I shared for a few years are in reality only the basis for, or prelude to, or earthly appearance of, two unimaginable, supercosmic, eternal somethings. Those somethings could be pictured as spheres or globes. Where the plane of Nature cuts through them—that is, in earthly life—they appear as two circles (circles are slices of spheres). Two circles that touched. But those two circles, above all the point at which they touched, are the very thing I am mourning for, homesick for, famished for. You tell me, "she goes on." But my heart and body are crying out, come back, come back. Be a circle, touching my circle on the plane of Nature. But I know this is impossible. I know that the thing I want is exactly the thing I can never get. The old life, the jokes, the drinks, the arguments, the love-making, the tiny, heartbreaking common-place. On any view whatever, to say "H. is dead," is to say "All that is gone." It is a part of the past. And the past is the past and that is what time means, and time itself is one more name for death, and Heaven it-self is a state where "the former things have passed away."

Talk to me about the truth of religion and I'll listen gladly. Talk to me about the duty of religion and I'll listen submissively. But don't come talking to me about the conso-lations of religion or I shall suspect that you don't understand.

Unless, of course, you can literally believe all that stuff about family reunions "on the further shore," pictured in entirely earthly terms. But that is all unscriptural, all out of bad hymns and lithographs. There's not a word of it in the Bible. And it rings false. We *know* it couldn't be like that. Reality never repeats. The exact same thing is never taken away and given back. How well the Spiritualists bait their hook! "Things on this side are not so different after all." There are cigars in Heaven. For that is what we should all like. The happy past restored.

And that, just that, is what I cry out for, with mad, midnight endearments and entreaties spoken into the empty air.

And poor C. quotes to me, "Do not mourn like those that have no hope." It astonishes me, the way we are invited to apply to ourselves words so obviously addressed to our betters. What St. Paul says can comfort only those who love God better than the dead, and the dead better than themselves. If a mother is mourning not for what she has lost but for what her dead child has lost, it is a comfort to believe that the child has not lost the end for which it was created. And it is a comfort to believe that she herself, in losing her chief or only natural happiness, has not lost a greater thing, that she may still hope to "glorify God and enjoy Him forever." A comfort to the God-aimed, eternal spirit within her. But not to her motherhood. The specifically maternal happiness must be written off. Never, in any place or time, will she have her son on her knees, or bathe him, or tell him a story, or plan for his future, or see her grandchild.

They tell me H. is happy now, they tell me she is at peace. What makes them so sure of this? I don't mean that I fear the worst of all. Nearly her last words were "I am at peace with God." She had not always been. And she never lied. And she wasn't easily deceived; least of all, in her own favor. I don't mean that. But why are they so sure that all anguish ends with death? More than half the Christian world, and millions in the

East, believe otherwise. How do they know she is "at rest." Why should the separation (if nothing else) which so agonizes the lover who is left behind be painless to the lover who departs?

"Because she is in God's hands." But if so, she was in God's hands all the time, and I have seen what they did to her here. Do they suddenly become gentler to us the moment we are out of the body? And if so, why? If God's goodness is inconsistent with hurting us, then either God is not good or there is no God: for in the only life we know He hurts us beyond our worst fears and beyond all we can imagine. If it is consistent with hurting us, then He may hurt us after death as unendurably as before it.

Sometimes it is hard not to say, "God forgive God." Sometimes it is hard to say so much. But if our faith is true, He didn't. He crucified Him.

Come, what do we gain by evasions? We are under the harrow and can't escape. Reality, looked at steadily, is unbearable. And how or why did such a reality blos/ som (or fester) here and there into the terrible phenomenon called consciousness? Why did it produce things like us who can see it and, seeing it, recoil in loathing? Who (stranger still) want to see it and take pains to find it out, even when no need compels them and even though the sight of it makes an incurable ulcer in their hearts? People like H. herself, who would have truth at any price.

If H. "is not," then she never was. I mistook a cloud of atoms for a person. There aren't, and never were, any people. Death only re/ veals the vacuity that was always there. What we call the living are simply those who have not yet been unmasked. All equally bankrupt, but some not yet declared.

But this must be nonsense; vacuity revealed to whom? bankruptcy declared to whom? To other boxes of fireworks or clouds of atoms. I will never believe—more strictly I can't believe—that one set of physical events could be, or make, a mistake about other sets.

No, my real fear is not of materialism. If it were true, we—or what we mistake for "we" —could get out, get from under the harrow. An overdose of sleeping pills would do it. I am more afraid that we are really rats in a trap. Or, worse still, rats in a laboratory. Someone said, I believe, "God always geometrizes." Supposing the truth were "God always vivisects"?

Sooner or later I must face the question in plain language. What reason have we, except our own desperate wishes, to believe that God is, by any standard we can conceive, "good"? Doesn't all the *prima facie* evidence suggest exactly the opposite? What have we to set against it?

We set Christ against it. But how if He were mistaken? Almost His last words may have a perfectly clear meaning. He had found that the Being He called Father was horribly and infinitely different from what He had supposed. The trap, so long and carefully prepared and so subtly baited, was at last sprung, on the cross. The vile practical joke had succeeded.

What chokes every prayer and every hope is the memory of all the prayers H. and I offered and all the false hopes we had. Not hopes raised merely by our own wishful thinking; hopes encouraged, even forced upon us, by false diagnoses, by X-ray photographs, by strange remissions, by one temporary recovery that might have ranked as a miracle. Step by step we were "led up the garden path." Time after time, when He seemed most gracious He was really preparing the next torture.

I wrote that last night. It was a yell rather than a thought. Let me try it over again. Is it rational to believe in a bad God? Anyway, in a God so bad as all that? The Cosmic Sadist, the spiteful imbecile?

I think it is, if nothing else, too anthropomorphic. When you come to think of it, it is far more anthropomorphic than picturing Him as a grave old king with a long beard. That image is a Jungian archetype. It links God with all the wise old kings in the fairy tales, with prophets, sages, magicians. Though it is (formally) the picture of a man, it suggests something more than humanity. At the very least it gets in the idea of something older than yourself, something that knows more, something you can't fathom. It preserves mystery. Therefore room for hope. Therefore room for a dread or awe that needn't be mere fear of mischief from a spiteful potentate. But the picture I was building up last night is simply the picture of a man like S.C.—who used to sit next to me at dinner and tell me what he'd been doing to the cats that afternoon. Now a being like S.C., however magnified, couldn't invent or create or govern anything. He would set traps and try to bait them. But he'd never have thought of baits like love, or laughter, or daffodils, or a frosty sunset. *He* make a universe? He couldn't make a joke, or a bow, or an apology, or a friend.

Or could one seriously introduce the idea of a bad God, as it were by the back door, through a sort of extreme Calvinism? You could say we are fallen and depraved. We are so depraved that our ideas of goodness count for nothing; or worse than nothing— the very fact that we think something good is presumptive evidence that it is really bad.

Now God has in fact—our worst fears are true—all the characteristics we regard as bad: unreasonableness, vanity, vindictive, ness, injustice, cruelty. But all these blacks (as they seem to us) are really whites. It's only our depravity makes them look black to us.

And so what? This, for all practical (and speculative) purposes sponges God off the slate. The word *good*, applied to Him, be, comes meaningless: like abracadabra. We have no motive for obeying Him. Not even fear. It is true we have His threats and prom, ises. But why should we believe them? If cruelty is from His point of view "good," telling lies may be "good" too. Even if they are true, what then? If His ideas of good are so very different from ours, what He calls "Heaven" might well be what we should call Hell, and vice, versa. Finally, if reality at its very root is so meaningless to us—or, putting it the other way round, if we are such total imbeciles—what is the point of trying to think either about God or about anything else? This knot comes undone when you try to pull it tight.

Why do I make room in my mind for such filth and nonsense? Do I hope that if feeling disguises itself as thought I shall feel less? Aren't all these notes the senseless writhings of a man who won't accept the fact that there is nothing we can do with suffering except to suffer it? Who still thinks there is some device (if only he could find it) which will make pain not to be pain. It doesn't really matter whether you grip the arms of the dentist's chair or let your hands lie in your lap. The drill drills on.

And grief still feels like fear. Perhaps, more strictly, like suspense. Or like waiting; just hanging about waiting for something to happen. It gives life a permanently provi‑sional feeling. It doesn't seem worth starting anything. I can't settle down. I yawn, I fidget, I smoke too much. Up till this I always had too little time. Now there is nothing but time. Almost pure time, empty successiveness.

One flesh. Or, if you prefer, one ship. The starboard engine has gone. I, the port engine, must chug along somehow till we make harbor. Or rather, till the journey ends. How can I assume a harbor? A lee shore, more likely, a black night, a deafening gale, breakers ahead—and any lights shown from the land probably being waved by wreckers. Such was H.'s landfall. Such was my mother's. I say their landfalls; not their arrivals.

III

IT'S NOT true that I'm always thinking of H. Work and conversation make that impossible. But the times when I'm not are perhaps my worst. For then, though I have forgotten the reason, there is spread over everything a vague sense of wrongness, of something amiss. Like in those dreams where nothing terrible occurs—nothing that would sound even remarkable if you told it at breakfast-time—but the atmosphere, the taste, of the whole thing is deadly. So with this. I see the rowan berries reddening and don't know for a moment why they, of all things, should be depressing. I hear a clock strike and some quality it always had before has gone out of the sound. What's wrong with the world to make it so flat, shabby, worn-out looking? Then I remember.

This is one of the things I'm afraid of. The agonies, the mad midnight moments, must, in the course of nature, die away. But what will follow? Just this apathy, this dead flatness? Will there come a time when I no longer ask why the world is like a mean street, because I shall take the squalor as normal? Does grief finally subside into boredom tinged by faint nausea?

Feelings, and feelings, and feelings. Let me try thinking instead. From the rational point of view, what new factor has H.'s death introduced into the problem of the universe? What grounds has it given me for doubting all that I believe? I knew already that these things, and worse, happened daily. I would have said that I had taken them into account. I had been warned—I had warned myself—not to reckon on worldly happiness. We were even promised sufferings. They were part of the program. We were even told, "Blessed are they that mourn," and I accepted it. I've got nothing that I hadn't bargained for. Of course it is different when the thing happens to oneself, not to others, and in reality, not in imagination. Yes; but should it, for a sane man, make quite such a difference as this? No. And it wouldn't for a man whose faith had been real faith and whose concern for other people's sorrows had been real concern. The case is too plain. If my house has collapsed at one blow, that is because it was a house of cards. The faith which "took these things into account" was not faith but imagination. The taking them into account was not real sympathy. If I had really cared, as I thought I did, about the sorrows of the world, I should not have been so overwhelmed when my own sorrow came. It has been an imaginary faith playing with innocuous counters labelled "Illness," "Pain," "Death," and "Loneliness." I thought I trusted the rope until it mattered to me whether it would bear me. Now it matters, and I find I didn't.

Bridge-players tell me that there must be some money on the game, "or else people won't take it seriously." Apparently it's like that. Your bid—for God or no God, for a good God or the Cosmic Sadist, for eternal life or nonentity—will not be serious if nothing much is staked on it. And you will never discover how serious it was until the stakes are raised horribly high; until you find that you are playing not for counters or for sixpences but for every penny you have in the world. Nothing less will shake a man —or at any rate a man like me—out of his merely verbal thinking and his merely notional beliefs. He has to be knocked silly before he comes to his senses. Only torture will bring out the truth. Only under torture does he discover it himself.

And I must surely admit—H. would have forced me to admit in a few passes—that, if my house was a house of cards, the sooner it was knocked down the better. And only suffering could do it. But then the Cosmic Sadist and Eternal Vivisector becomes an unnecessary hypothesis.

Is this last note a sign that I'm incurable, that when reality smashes my dream to bits, I mope and snarl while the first shock lasts, and then patiently, idiotically, start putting it together again? And so always? However often the house of cards falls, shall I set about rebuilding it? Is that what I'm doing now?

Indeed it's likely enough that what I shall call, if it happens, a "restoration of faith" will turn out to be only one more house of cards. And I shan't know whether it is or not until the next blow comes—when, say, fatal disease is diagnosed in my body too, or war breaks out, or I have ruined myself by some ghastly mistake in my work. But there are two questions here. In which sense may it be a house of cards? Because the things I am believing are only a dream, or because I only dream that I believe them?

As for the things themselves, why should the thoughts I had a week ago be any more trustworthy than the better thoughts I have now? I am surely, in general, a saner man than I was then. Why should the desperate imaginings of a man dazed—I said it was like being concussed—be especially reliable?

Because there was no wishful thinking in them? Because, being so horrible, they were therefore all the more likely to be true? But there are fear-fulfillment as well as wish-fulfillment dreams. And were they wholly distasteful? No. In a way I liked them. I am even aware of a slight reluctance to accept the opposite thoughts. All that stuff about the Cosmic Sadist was not so much the expression of thought as of hatred. I was getting from it the only pleasure a man in anguish can get; the pleasure of hitting back. It was really just Billingsgate—mere abuse; "telling God what I thought of Him." And of course, as in all abusive language, "what I thought" didn't mean what I thought true. Only what I thought would offend Him (and His worshippers) most. That sort of thing is never said without some pleasure. Gets it "off your chest." You feel better for a moment.

But the mood is no evidence. Of course the cat will growl and spit at the operator and bite him if she can. But the real question is whether he is a vet or a vivisector. Her bad language throws no light on it one way or the other.

And I can believe He is a vet when I think of my own suffering. It is harder when I think of hers. What is grief compared with physical pain? Whatever fools may say, the body can suffer twenty times more than the mind. The mind has always some power of evasion. At worst, the unbearable thought only comes back and back, but the physical pain can be absolutely continuous. Grief is like a bomber circling round and dropping its bombs each time the circle brings it overhead; physical pain is like the steady barrage on a trench in World War One, hours of it with no let-up for a moment. Thought is never static; pain often is.

What sort of a lover am I to think so much about my affliction and so much less about hers? Even the insane call, "Come back," is all for my own sake. I never even raised the question whether such a return, if it were possible, would be good for her. I want her back as an ingredient in the restoration of *my* past. Could I have wished her anything worse? Having got once through death, to come back and then, at some later date, have all her dying to do over again? They call Stephen the first martyr. Hadn't Lazarus the rawer deal?

I begin to see. My love for H. was of much the same quality as my faith in God. I won't exaggerate, though. Whether there was anything but imagination in the faith, or anything but egoism in the love, God knows. I don't. There may have been a little more; especially in my love for H. But neither was the thing I thought it was. A good deal of the card-castle about both.

What does it matter how this grief of mine evolves or what I do with it? What does it matter how I remember her or whether I remember her at all? None of these alternatives will either ease or aggravate her past anguish.

Her past anguish. How do I know that all her anguish is past? I never believed before —I thought it immensely improbable—that the faithfulest soul could leap straight into perfection and peace the moment death has rattled in the throat. It would be wishful thinking with a vengeance to take up that belief now. H. was a splendid thing; a soul straight, bright, and tempered like a sword. But not a perfected saint. A sinful woman married to a sinful man; two of God's patients, not yet cured. I know there are not only tears to be dried but stains to be scoured. The sword will be made even brighter.

But oh God, tenderly, tenderly. Already, month by month and week by week you broke her body on the wheel whilst she still wore it. Is it not yet enough?

The terrible thing is that a perfectly good God is in this matter hardly less formidable than a Cosmic Sadist. The more we believe that God hurts only to heal, the less we can believe that there is any use in begging for tenderness. A cruel man might be bribed—

might grow tired of his vile sport—might have a temporary fit of mercy, as alcoholics have fits of sobriety. But suppose that what you are up against is a surgeon whose intentions are wholly good. The kinder and more conscientious he is, the more inexorably he will go on cutting. If he yielded to your entreaties, if he stopped before the operation was complete, all the pain up to that point would have been useless. But is it credible that such extremities of torture should be necessary for us? Well, take your choice. The tortures occur. If they are unnecessary, then there is no God or a bad one. If there is a good God, then these tortures are necessary. For no even moderately good Being could possibly inflict or permit them if they weren't.

Either way, we're for it.

What do people mean when they say, "I am not afraid of God because I know He is good?" Have they never even been to a dentist?

Yet this is unendurable. And then one babbles—"If only I could bear it, or the worst of it, or any of it, instead of her." But one can't tell how serious that bid is, for nothing is staked on it. If it suddenly became a real possibility, then, for the first time, we should discover how seriously we had meant it. But is it ever allowed?

It was allowed to One, we are told, and I find I can now believe again, that He has done vicariously whatever can be so done. He replies to our babble, "You cannot and you dare not. I could and dared."

Something quite unexpected has happened. It came this morning early. For various reasons, not in themselves at all mysterious, my heart was lighter than it had been for many weeks. For one thing, I suppose I am recovering physically from a good deal of mere exhaustion. And I'd had a very tiring but very healthy twelve hours the day before, and a sounder night's sleep; and after ten days of low-hung gray skies and motionless warm dampness, the sun was shining and there was a light breeze. And suddenly at the very moment when, so far, I mourned H. least, I remembered her best. Indeed it was something (almost) better than memory; an instantaneous, unanswerable impression. To say it was like a meeting would be going too far. Yet there was that in it which tempts one to use those words. It was as if the lifting of the sorrow removed a barrier.

Why has no one told me these things? How easily I might have misjudged another man in the same situation? I might have said, "He's got over it. He's forgotten his wife," when the truth was, "He remembers her better *because* he has partly got over it."

Such was the fact. And I believe I can make sense out of it. You can't see anything properly while your eyes are blurred with tears. You can't, in most things, get what you want if you want it too desperately: anyway, you can't get the best out of it. "Now! Let's have a real good talk" reduces everyone to silence, "I *must* get a good sleep tonight" ushers in hours of wakefulness. Delicious drinks are wasted on a really ravenous thirst. Is it similarly the very intensity of the longing that draws the iron curtain, that makes us feel we are staring into a vacuum when we think about our dead? "Them as asks" (at any rate "as asks too importunately") don't get. Perhaps can't.

And so, perhaps, with God. I have gradually been coming to feel that the door is no longer shut and bolted. Was it my own frantic need that slammed it in my face? The time when there is nothing at all in your soul except a cry for help may be just the time when God can't give it: you are like the drowning man who can't be helped because he clutches and grabs. Perhaps your own reiterated cries deafen you to the voice you hoped to hear.

On the other hand, "Knock and it shall be opened." But does knocking mean hammering and kicking the door like a maniac? And there's also "To him that hath shall be given." After all, you must have a capacity to receive, or even omnipotence can't give. Perhaps your own passion temporarily destroys the capacity.

For all sorts of mistakes are possible when you are dealing with Him. Long ago, before we were married, H. was haunted all one morning as she went about her work with the obscure sense of God (so to speak) "at her elbow," demanding her attention. And of course, not being a perfected saint, she had the feeling that it would be a question, as it usually is, of some unrepented sin or tedious duty. At last she gave in—I know how one puts it off—and faced Him. But the message was "I want to *give* you something," and instantly she entered into joy.

I think I am beginning to understand why grief feels like suspense. It comes from the frustration of so many impulses that had become habitual. Thought after thought, feeling after feeling, action after action, had H. for their object. Now their target is gone. I keep on through habit fitting an arrow to the string; then I remember and have to lay the bow down. So many roads lead thought to H. I set out on one of them. But now there's an impassable frontier-post across it. So many roads once; now so many *culs de sac*.

For a good wife contains so many persons in herself. What was H. not to me? She was my daughter and my mother, my pupil and my teacher, my subject and my sovereign;

and always, holding all these in solution, my trusty comrade, friend, shipmate, fellow-soldier. My mistress; but at the same time all that any man friend (and I have good ones) has ever been to me. Perhaps more. If we had never fallen in love we should have none the less been always together, and created a scandal. That's what I meant when I once praised her for her "masculine virtues." But she soon put a stop to that by asking how I'd like to be praised for my feminine ones. It was a good *riposte*, dear. Yet there was something of the Amazon, something of Penthesileia and Camilla. And you, as well as I, were glad it should be there. You were glad I should recognize it.

Solomon calls his bride Sister. Could a woman be a complete wife unless, for a moment, in one particular mood, a man felt almost inclined to call her Brother?

"It was too perfect to last," so I am tempted

to say of our marriage. But it can be meant in two ways. It may be grimly pessimistic— as if God no sooner saw two of His creatures happy than He stopped it ("None of that here!"). As if He were like the Hostess at the sherry-party who separates two guests the moment they show signs of having got into a real conversation. But it could also mean "This had reached its proper perfection. This had become what it had in it to be. Therefore of course it would not be prolonged." As if God said, "Good; you have mastered that exercise. I am very pleased with it. And now you are ready to go on to the next." When you have learned to do quadratics and enjoy doing them you will not be set them much longer. The teacher moves you on.

For we did learn and achieve something. There is, hidden or flaunted, a sword between the sexes till an entire marriage reconciles them. It is arrogance in us to call frankness, fairness, and chivalry "masculine" when we see them in a woman; it is arrogance in them, to describe a man's sensitiveness or tact or tenderness as "feminine." But also what poor, warped fragments of humanity most mere men and mere women must be to make the implications of that arrogance plausible. Marriage heals this. Jointly the two become fully human. "In the image of God created He *them*." Thus, by a paradox, this carnival of sexuality leads us out beyond our sexes.

And then one or other dies. And we think of this as love cut short; like a dance stopped in mid-career or a flower with its head unluckily snapped off—something truncated and therefore, lacking its due shape. I wonder. If, as I can't help suspecting, the dead also feel the pains of separation (and this may be one of their purgatorial sufferings), then for both lovers, and for all pairs of lovers without exception, bereavement is a universal and integral part of our experience of love. It follows marriage as normally as marriage follows courtship or as autumn follows summer. It is not a truncation of the process but one of its phases; not the interruption of the dance, but the next figure. We are "taken out of ourselves" by the loved one while she is here. Then comes the tragic figure of the dance in which we must learn to be still taken out of ourselves though the bodily presence is withdrawn, to love the very Her, and not fall back to loving our past, or our memory, or our sorrow, or our relief from sorrow, or our own love.

Looking back, I see that only a very little time ago I was greatly concerned about my memory of H. and how false it might become. For some reason—the merciful good sense of God is the only one I can think of— I have stopped bothering about that. And the remarkable thing is that since I stopped bothering about it, she seems to meet me everywhere. *Meet* is far too strong a word. I don't mean anything remotely like an apparition or a voice. I don't mean even any strikingly emotional experience at any particular moment. Rather, a sort of unobtrusive but massive sense that she is, just as much as ever, a fact to be taken into account.

"To be taken into account" is perhaps an unfortunate way of putting it. It sounds as if she were rather a battle-axe. How can I put it better? Would "momentously real" or "obstinately real" do? It is as if the experience said to me, "You are, as it happens, extremely glad that H. is still a fact. But remember she would be equally a fact whether you liked it or not. Your preferences have not been considered."

How far have I got? Just as far, I think, as a widower of another sort who would stop, leaning on his spade, and say in answer to our inquiry, "Thank 'ee. Mustn't grumble.

I do miss her something dreadful. But they say these things are sent to try us." We have come to the same point; he with his spade, and I, who am not now much good at digging, with my own instrument. But of course one must take "sent to try us" the right way. God has not been trying an experiment on my faith or love in order to find out their quality. He knew it already. It was I who didn't. In this trial He makes us occupy the dock, the witness box, and the bench all at once. He always knew that my temple was a house of cards. His only way of making me realize the fact was to knock it down.

Getting over it so soon? But the words are ambiguous. To say the patient is getting over it after an operation for appendicitis is one thing; after he's had his leg off it is quite another. After that operation either the wounded stump heals or the man dies. If it heals, the fierce, continuous pain will stop.

Presently he'll get back his strength and be able to stump about on his wooden leg. He has "got over it." But he will probably have recurrent pains in the stump all his life, and perhaps pretty bad ones; and he will always be a one-legged man. There will be hardly any moment when he forgets it. Bathing, dressing, sitting down and getting up again, even lying in bed, will all be different. His whole way of life will be changed. All sorts of pleasures and activities that he once took for granted will have to be simply written off. Duties too. At present I am learning to get about on crutches. Perhaps I shall presently be given a wooden leg. But I shall never be a biped again.

Still, there's no denying that in some sense I "feel better," and with that comes at once a sort of shame, and a feeling that one is under a sort of obligation to cherish and foment and prolong one's unhappiness. I've read about that in books, but I never dreamed I should feel it myself. I am sure H. wouldn't approve of it. She'd tell me not to be a fool. So I'm pretty certain, would God. What is behind it?

Partly, no doubt, vanity. We want to prove to ourselves that we are lovers on the grand scale, tragic heroes; not just ordinary privates in the huge army of the bereaved, slogging along and making the best of a bad job. But that's not the whole of the explanation.

I think there is also a confusion. We don't really want grief, in its first agonies, to be prolonged: nobody could. But we want something else of which grief is a frequent symptom, and then we confuse the symptom with the thing itself. I wrote the other night that bereavement is not the truncation of married love but one of its regular phases —like the honeymoon. What we want is to live our marriage well and faithfully through that phase too. If it hurts (and it certainly will) we accept the pains as a necessary part of this phase. We don't want to escape them at the price of desertion or divorce. Killing the dead a second time. We were one flesh. Now that it has been cut in two, we don't want to pretend that it is whole and complete. We will be still married, still in love. Therefore we shall still ache. But we are not at all—if we understand ourselves—seeking the aches for their own sake. The less of them the better, so long as the marriage is preserved. And the more joy there can be in the marriage between dead and living, the better.

The better in every way. For, as I have discovered, passionate grief does not link us with the dead but cuts us off from them. This becomes clearer and clearer. It is just at those moments when I feel least sorrow—getting into my morning bath is usually one of them—that H. rushes upon my mind in her full reality, her otherness. Not, as in my worst moments, all foreshortened and patheticized and solemnized by my miseries, but as she is in her own right. This is good and tonic.

I seem to remember—though I couldn't quote one at the moment—all sorts of ballads and folk-tales in which the dead tell us that our mourning does them some kind of wrong. They beg us to stop it. There may be far more depth in this than I thought. If so, our grandfather's generation went very far astray. All that (sometimes lifelong) ritual of sorrow—visiting graves, keeping anniversaries, leaving the empty bedroom exactly as "the departed" used to keep it, mentioning the dead either not at all or always in a special voice, or even (like Queen Victoria) having the dead man's clothes put out for dinner every evening—this was like mummification. It made the dead far more dead.

Or was that (unconsciously) its purpose? Something very primitive may be at work here. To keep the dead thoroughly dead, to make sure that they won't come sidling back among the living, is a main pre-occupation of the savage mind. At all costs make them "stay put." Certainly these rituals do in fact emphasize their deadness. Perhaps this result was not really so unwelcome, not always, as the ritualists believed.

But I've no business to judge them. All guess-work; I'd better keep my breath to cool my own porridge. For me at any rate the program is plain. I will turn to her as often as possible in gladness. I will even salute her with a laugh. The less I mourn her the nearer I seem to her.

An admirable program. Unfortunately it can't be carried out. Tonight all the hells of young grief have opened again; the mad words, the bitter resentment, the fluttering in the stomach, the nightmare unreality, the wallowed-in tears. For in grief nothing "stays put." One keeps on emerging from a phase, but it always recurs. Round and round. Everything repeats. Am I going in circles, or dare I hope I am on a spiral?

But if a spiral, am I going up or down it?

How often—will it be for always?—how often will the vast emptiness astonish me like a complete novelty and make me say, "I never realized my loss till this moment"? The same leg is cut off time after time. The first plunge of the knife into the flesh is felt again and again.

They say "The coward dies many times;" so does the beloved. Didn't the eagle find a fresh liver to tear in Prometheus every time it dined?

IV

This is the fourth—and the last—empty MS. book I can find in the house; at least nearly empty, for there are some pages of very ancient arithmetic at the end by J. I resolve to let this limit my jottings. I *will not* start buying books for the purpose. In so far as this record was a defense against total collapse, a safety valve, it has done some good. The other end I had in view turns out to have been based on a misunderstanding. I thought I could describe a *state*; make a map of sorrow. Sorrow, however, turns out to be not a state but a process. It needs not a map but a history, and if I don't stop writing that history at some quite arbitrary point, there's no reason why I should ever stop. There is something new to be chronicled every day. Grief is like a long valley, a winding valley where any bend may reveal a totally new landscape. As I've already noted, not every bend does. Sometimes the surprise is the opposite one; you are presented with exactly the same sort of country you thought you had left behind miles ago. That is when you wonder whether the valley isn't a circular trench. But it isn't. There are partial recurrences, but the sequence doesn't repeat.

Here, for instance, is a new phase, a new loss. I do all the walking I can, for I'd be a fool to go to bed not tired. Today I have been revisiting old haunts, taking one of the long rambles that made me so happy in my bachelor days. And this time the face of nature was not emptied of its beauty and the world didn't look (as I complained some days ago) like a mean street. On the contrary, every horizon, every stile or clump of trees, summoned me into a past kind of happiness, my pre-H. happiness. But the invitation seemed to me horrible. The happiness into which it invited me was insipid. I find that I don't want to go back again and be happy in *that* way. It frightens me to think that a mere going back should even be possible. For this fate would seem to me the worst of all; to reach a state in which my years of love and marriage should appear in retrospect a charming episode—like a holiday—that had briefly interrupted my interminable life and returned me to normal, unchanged. And then it would come to seem unreal—something so foreign to the usual texture of my history that I could almost believe it had happened to someone else. Thus H. would die to me a second time; a worse bereavement than the first. Anything but that.

Did you ever know, dear, how much you took away with you when you left? You have stripped me even of my past, even of the things we never shared. I was wrong to say the stump was recovering from the pain of the amputation. I was deceived because it has so many ways to hurt me that I discover them only one by one.

Still, there are the two enormous gains—I know myself too well now to call them "lasting." Turned to God, my mind no longer meets that locked door; turned to H., it no longer meets that vacuum—nor all that fuss about my mental image of her. My jottings show something of the process, but not so much as I'd hoped. Perhaps both changes were really not observable. There was no sudden, striking, and emotional transition. Like the warming of a room or the coming of daylight. When you first notice them they have already been going on for some time.

The notes have been about myself, and about H., and about God. In that order.

The order and the proportions exactly what they ought not to have been. And I see that I have nowhere fallen into that mode of thinking about either which we call praising them. Yet that would have been best for me. Praise is the mode of love which always has some element of joy in it. Praise in due order; of Him as the giver, of her as the gift. Don't we in praise somehow enjoy what we praise, however far we are from it? I must do more of this. I have lost the fruition I once had of H. And I am far, far away in the valley of my unlikeness, from the fruition which, if His mercies are infinite, I may some time have of God. But by praising I can still, in some degree, enjoy her, and already, in some degree, enjoy Him. Better than nothing.

But perhaps I lack the gift. I see I've described H. as being like a sword. That's true as far as it goes. But utterly inadequate by itself, and misleading. I ought to have balanced it. I ought to have said, "But also like a garden. Like a nest of gardens, wall within wall, hedge within hedge, more secret, more full of fragrant and fertile life, the further you entered."

And then, of her, and of every created thing I praise, I should say, "In some way, in its unique way, like Him who made it."

Thus up from the garden to the Gardener, from the sword to the Smith. To the life-giving Life and the Beauty that makes beautiful.

"She is in God's hand." That gains a new energy when I think of her as a sword. Perhaps the earthly life I shared with her was only part of the tempering. Now perhaps He grasps the hilt; weighs the new weapon; makes lightnings with it in the air. "A right Jerusalem blade."

One moment last night can be described in similes; otherwise it won't go into language at all. Imagine a man in total darkness. He thinks he is in a cellar or dungeon. Then there comes a sound. He thinks it might be a sound from far off—waves or wind-blown trees or cattle half a mile away. And if so, it proves he's not in a cellar, but free, in the open air. Or it may be a much smaller sound close at hand—a chuckle of laughter. And if so, there is a friend just beside him in the dark. Either way, a good, good sound. I'm not mad enough to take such an experience as evidence for anything. It is simply the leaping into imaginative activity of an idea which I would always have theoretically admitted—the idea that I, or any mortal at any time, may be utterly mistaken as to the situation he is really in.

Five senses; an incurably abstract intellect; a haphazardly selective memory; a set of preconceptions and assumptions so numerous that I can never examine more than a minority of them—never become even conscious of them all. How much of total reality can such an apparatus let through?

I will not, if I can help it, shin up either the feathery or the prickly tree. Two widely different convictions press more and more on my mind. One is that the Eternal Vet is even more inexorable and the possible operations even more painful than our severest imaginings can forbode. But the other, that "all shall be well, and all shall be well, and all manner of thing shall be well."

It doesn't matter that all the photographs of H. are bad. It doesn't matter—not much—if my memory of her is imperfect. Images, whether on paper or in the mind, are not important for themselves. Merely links. Take a parallel from an infinitely higher sphere. Tomorrow morning a priest will give me a little round, thin, cold, tasteless wafer. Is it a disadvantage—is it not in some ways an advantage—that it can't pretend the least *resemblance* to that with which it unites me?

I need Christ, not something that resembles Him. I want H., not something that is like her. A really good photograph might become in the end a snare, a horror, and an obstacle.

Images, I must suppose, have their use or they would not have been so popular. (It makes little difference whether they are pictures and statues outside the mind or imaginative constructions within it.) To me, however, their danger is more obvious. Images of the Holy easily become holy images—sacrosanct. My idea of God is not a divine idea. It has to be shattered time after time. He shatters it Himself. He is the great iconoclast. Could we not almost say that this shattering is one of the marks of His presence? The Incarnation is the supreme example; it leaves all previous ideas of the Messiah in ruins. And most are "offended" by the iconoclasm; and blessed are those who are not. But the same thing happens in our private prayers.

All reality is iconoclastic. The earthly beloved, even in this life, incessantly triumphs over your mere idea of her. And you want her to; you want her with all her resistances, all her faults, all her unexpectedness. That is, in her foursquare and independent reality. And this, not any image or memory, is what we are to love still, after she is dead.

But "this" is not now imaginable. In that respect H. and all the dead are like God. In that respect loving her has become, in its measure, like loving Him. In both cases I must stretch out the arms and hands of love—its eyes cannot here be used—to the reality, through—across—all the changeful phantasmagoria of my thoughts, passions, and imaginings. I mustn't sit down content with the phantasmagoria itself and worship that for Him, or love that for her.

Not my idea of God, but God. Not my idea of H., but H. Yes, and also not my idea of my neighbor, but my neighbor. For don't we often make this mistake as regards people who are still alive—who are with us in the same room? Talking and acting not to the man himself but to the picture—almost the *précis*—we've made of him in our own minds? And he has to depart from it pretty widely before we even notice the fact. In real life—that's one way it differs from novels—his words and acts are, if we observe closely, hardly ever quite "in character," that is, in what we call his character. There's always a card in his hand we didn't know about.

My reason for assuming that I do this to other people is the fact that so often I find them obviously doing it to me. We all think we've got one another taped.

And all this time I may, once more, be building with cards. And if I am He will once more knock the building flat. He will knock it down as often as proves necessary. Unless I have to be finally given up as hopeless, and left building pasteboard palaces in Hell forever; "free among the dead."

Am I, for instance, just sidling back to God because I know that if there's any road to H., it runs through Him? But then of course I know perfectly well that He can't be used as a road. If you're approaching Him not as the goal but as a road, not as the end but as a means, you're not really approaching Him at all. That's what was really wrong with all those popular pictures of happy reunions "on the further shore;" not the simple-minded and very earthly images, but the fact that they make an End of what we can get only as a by-product of the true End.

Lord, are these your real terms? Can I meet H. again only if I learn to love you so much that I don't care whether I meet her or not? Consider, Lord, how it looks to us. What would anyone think of me if I said to the boys, "No toffee now. But when you've grown up and don't really want toffee you shall have as much of it as you choose?"

If I knew that to be eternally divided from H. and eternally forgotten by her would add a greater joy and splendor to her being, of course I'd say, "Fire ahead." Just as if, on earth, I could have cured her cancer by never seeing her again, I'd have arranged never to see her again. I'd have had to. Any decent person would. But that's quite different. That's not the situation I'm in.

When I lay these questions before God I get no answer. But a rather special sort of "No answer." It is not the locked door. It is more like a silent, certainly not uncompassionate, gaze. As though He shook His head not in refusal but waiving the question. Like, "Peace, child; you don't understand."

Can a mortal ask questions which God finds unanswerable? Quite easily, I should think. All nonsense questions are unanswerable. How many hours are there in a mile? Is yellow square or round? Probably half the questions we ask—half our great theological and metaphysical problems—are like that.

And now that I come to think of it, there's no practical problem before me at all. I know the two great commandments, and I'd better get on with them. Indeed, H.'s death has ended the practical problem. While she was alive I could, in practice, have put her before God; that is, could have done what she wanted instead of what He wanted; if there'd been a conflict. What's left is not a problem about anything I could *do*. It's all about weights of feelings and motives and that sort of thing. It's a problem I'm setting myself. I don't believe God set it me at all.

The fruition of God. Reunion with the dead. These can't figure in my thinking except as counters. Blank checks. My idea—if you can call it an idea—of the first is a huge, risky extrapolation from a very few and short experiences here on earth. Probably not such valuable experiences as I think. Perhaps even of less value than others that I take no account of. My idea of the second is also an extrapolation. The reality of either—the cashing of either check—would probably blow all one's ideas about both (how much more one's ideas about their relations to each other) into smithereens.

The mystical union on the one hand. The resurrection of the body, on the other. I can't reach the ghost of an image, a formula, or even a feeling, that combines them. But the reality, we are given to understand, does. Reality the iconoclast once more. Heaven will solve our problems, but not, I think, by showing us subtle reconciliations between all our apparently contradictory notions. The notions will all be knocked from under our feet. We shall see that there never was any problem.

And, more than once, that impression which I can't describe except by saying that it's like the sound of a chuckle in the darkness. The sense that some shattering and disarming simplicity is the real answer.

It is often thought that the dead see us. And we assume, whether reasonably or not, that if they see us at all they see us more clearly than before. Does H. now see exactly how much froth or tinsel there was in what she called, and I call, my love? So be it. Look your hardest, dear. I wouldn't hide if I could. We didn't idealize each other. We tried to keep no secrets. You knew most of the rotten places in me already. If you now see anything worse, I can take it. So can you. Rebuke, explain, mock, forgive. For this is one of the miracles of love; it gives— to both, but perhaps especially to the woman—a power of seeing through its own enchantments and yet not being disenchanted.

To see, in some measure, like God. His love and His knowledge are not distinct from one another, nor from Him. We could almost say He sees because He loves, and therefore loves although He sees.

Sometimes, Lord, one is tempted to say that if you wanted us to behave like the lilies of the field you might have given us an organization more like theirs. But that, I suppose, is just your grand experiment. Or no; not an experiment, for you have no need to find things out. Rather your grand enterprise. To make an organism which is also a spirit; to make that terrible oxymoron, a "spiritual animal." To take a poor primate, a beast with nerve-endings all over it, a creature with a stomach that wants to be filled, a breeding animal that wants its mate, and say, "Now get on with it. Become a god."

I said, several notebooks ago, that even if I got what seemed like an assurance of H.'s presence, I wouldn't believe it. Easier said than done. Even now, though, I won't treat anything of that sort as evidence. It's the *quality* of last night's experience—not what it proves but what it was—that makes it worth putting down. It was quite incredibly unemotional. Just the impression of her *mind* momentarily facing my own. Mind, not "soul" as we tend to think of soul. Certainly the reverse of what is called "soulful." Not at all like a rapturous reunion of lovers. Much more like getting a telephone call or a wire from her about some practical arrangement. Not that there was any "message"—just intelligence and attention. No sense of joy or sorrow. No love even, in our ordinary sense. No un-love. I had never in any mood imagined the dead as being so— well, so business-like. Yet there was an extreme and cheerful intimacy. An intimacy that had not passed through the senses or the emotions at all.

If this was a throw-up from my unconscious, then my unconscious must be a far more interesting region than the depth psychologists have led me to expect. For one thing, it is apparently much less primitive than my consciousness.

Wherever it came from, it has made a sort of spring cleaning in my mind. The dead could be like that; sheer intellects. A Greek philosopher wouldn't have been surprised at an experience like mine. He would have expected that if anything of us remained

after death it would be just that. Up to now
this always seemed to me a most arid and
chilling idea. The absence of emotion re-
pelled me. But in this contact (whether real
or apparent) it didn't do anything of the
sort. One didn't need emotion. The intimacy was complete—sharply bracing and
restorative too—without it. Can that intimacy be love itself—always in this life at-
tended with emotion, not because it is itself
an emotion, or needs an attendant emotion,
but because our animal souls, our nervous
systems, our imaginations, have to respond
to it in that way? If so, how many preconceptions I must scrap! A society, a com-
munion, of pure intelligences would not be
cold, drab and comfortless. On the other
hand it wouldn't be very like what people
usually mean when they use such words as
"spiritual," or "mystical," or "holy." It
would, if I have had a glimpse, be—well,
I'm almost scared at the adjectives I'd have
to use. Brisk? cheerful? keen? alert? intense?

wide-awake? Above all, solid. Utterly reliable. Firm. There is no nonsense about
the dead.

When I say "intellect" I include will.
Attention is an act of will. Intelligence in
action is will *par excellence*. What seemed to
meet me was full of resolution.

Once very near the end I said, "If you can
—if it is allowed—come to me when I too
am on my death bed." "Allowed!" she said.
"Heaven would have a job to hold me; and
as for Hell, I'd break it into bits." She knew
she was speaking a kind of mythological
language, with even an element of comedy
in it. There was a twinkle as well as a tear
in her eye. But there was no myth and no
joke about the will, deeper than any feeling,
that flashed through her.

But I mustn't, because I have come to mis-
understand a little less completely what a

pure intelligence might be, lean over too far. There is also, whatever it means, the resurrection of the body. We cannot understand. The best is perhaps what we understand least.

Didn't people dispute once whether the final vision of God was more an act of intelligence or of love? That is probably another of the nonsense questions.

How wicked it would be, if we could, to call the dead back! She said not to me but to the chaplain, "I am at peace with God." She smiled, but not at me. *Poi si tornò all' eterna fontana.*

AFTERWORD

by

Chad Walsh

I SUPPOSE I knew C. S. Lewis about as well as any American did. Our lives touched at a number of points. These ranged from that day in the summer of 1948 when I first met him in Oxford, to another day in late 1961 when I again went to Oxford to see him, for the last time as it turned out. On other visits through the years, I saw him vigorous, buoyant, primed for intellectual debate. Toward the end of his life—he died the same day as President Kennedy, November 22, 1963—I saw him curiously quiet and in failing health. Perhaps four or five actual trips to England in all, and the chance to see Lewis—and yet I came to feel that we understood each other, that we were friends.

It all began during World War II, when a friend introduced me to Lewis's work with a copy of his philosophic science fiction novel, *Perelandra*. I could not put it down. I had always loved good science fiction, but never had I come on any as haunting; I was ready to take the next spacecraft to Venus and dwell on the sensuous, floating islands where the story takes place. I began reading everything of Lewis's I could lay hands on, and wrote him an ardent fan letter, to which he graciously replied in his own highly abbreviated handwriting. Thus began a steady correspondence that lasted through the years. I know now how many letters he received and how heavy a task it must have been to answer them; today I think with some guilt about the chore I, yet another American admirer, imposed upon him. But I cannot regret it. The letters eventually brought us together, face to face.

My memories also keep going back to that remarkable woman, Joy Davidman Gresham, whom Lewis eventually married after a long career as a confirmed bachelor. My wife and I had known her well for several years before she and Lewis met. This was another case of a fan letter leading to friendship, but I was the recipient this time. Joy and her husband, Bill, had come on my book, *C. S. Lewis: Apostle to the Skeptics,* and she wrote to me, as one Lewis enthusiast to another. The Greshams sounded interesting, and we invited them to visit us at our summer place in Vermont. We came to know them well and deeply love them—both of them, but especially Joy. When cancer claimed her after three years of happy marriage with Lewis, we sensed and could share some portion of the agony and loss that he experienced in his dark night of the soul.

Although Lewis died in the early 1960s, his fame and readership are experiencing a new surge. He was not a transient phenomenon. Many hundreds of thousands (and many of them young) are turning to his work not simply for an intelligent analysis of those perennial philosophic and religious questions that haunt mankind, but also for the sheer, literary pleasure that this superbly gifted writer can bestow. The *Narnia* stories, the science fiction trilogy, *The Screwtape Letters, Mere Christianity, The Great Divorce*—each Lewis enthusiast has his own priority list—are as fresh and new minted today as when they first saw print. The man who called himself a "dinosaur" in his address at Cambridge is proving as little timebound as any author of the century.

What kind of man was he? I think it is that question which compelled me to write a book about him. I *felt* I knew him from his books, and from his many letters. But a writer can easily wear a literary mask when he holds pen in hand. I wanted to know him, person to person, and to check that impression against those I had gained from his books. Lewis earnestly, even desperately, tried to dissuade me, via air mail, from doing the book. He insisted that only safely dead authors were worthy of scholarly attention.

But I persisted, and here I was in Oxford on a summer day of 1948. To be more precise, I was in the lobby of the King's Arms Hotel, where Lewis (once he saw I was determined to write the book) had kindly reserved a room for me. I kept thinking of the photos I had seen. They had a bluff and hardy look, a certain suggestion of solidity, eyes alive with intelligence.

What I did not expect to meet, when a Mr. Lewis was announced to me, was a man with a walrus mustache. And a man whose answers to my questions seemed just a shade confusing, as though I had made some mistake in phrasing them. In my fluster, it was some minutes before I realized that I was talking with Lewis's brother, Warren ("Warnie"), a retired army officer. Warnie had evidently been sent as a scout to examine the unknown American professor and decide what strategy was appropriate. Lewis valued his privacy and did not casually suffer it to be breached.

When I met C. S. Lewis soon afterward, his appearance and his manner seemed already familiar. He looked like his photos, though with a florid complexion that black-and-white photography could not suggest. His clothes had a casual and rumpled ease. There was something of an outdoors air about him, though most of his hours must have been spent indoors amid books.

In manner, he was straight to the point. He was not given to the sort of chitchat that simply fills in time, though in some moods he could take delight in a battle of verbal wit. I felt, however, that he did not work at it, and that his conversation, though always interesting, was less consistently brilliant than his writing. I soon learned to recognize when a conversation was boring him—as, for example, when I talked about politics. Once I shifted the topic to some literary, philosophic, or religious question, his eyes would come alive and he would throw himself into the conversation, which usually turned out to be a debate.

To him an ideal conversation was an intellectual fencing match, and may the man with the best dialectic win. The few times I crossed swords with him, he won. I also noticed that he seemed singularly uninterested in introspection. He found so many things outside himself interesting that he had no time to study himself. At least that was the impression that grew on me, though I had to modify it when, years later, I read *A Grief Observed*.

Lewis liked to contrast the two sides of his family. His father was a solicitor and the first Lewis to enter upon a professional career. Farther back in the line C. S. Lewis's great-grandfather was a Welsh farmer; the latter's son had emigrated to Ireland where he became a partner in a shipbuilding firm.

The mother's side, the Hamiltons, included many generations of lawyers, sailors, clergymen. A Norman knight, buried at Battle Abbey, was one of Mrs. Lewis's ancestors. Thus, two very different genealogies came together in C. S. Lewis. As he put it in *Surprised by Joy: The Shape of My Early Life:*[1]

> The two families from which I spring were as different in temperament as in origin. My father's people were true Welshmen, sentimental, passionate, and rhetorical, easily moved both to anger and to tenderness; men who laughed and cried a great deal and who had not much of the talent for happiness. The Hamiltons were a cooler race. Their minds were critical and ironic and they had the talent for happiness in a high degree— went straight for it as experienced travelers go for the best seat in a train. From my earliest years I was aware of the vivid contrast between my mother's cheerful and tranquil affection and the ups and downs of my father's emotional life, and this bred in me

1. (New York: Harcourt Brace World, 1955.)

long before I was old enough to give it a name a certain distrust or dislike of emotion as something uncomfortable and embarrassing and even dangerous.

To these very different parents, Clive Staples Lewis was born in a semi-detached house on the outskirts of Belfast, November 29, 1898. Preceding him by a little over three years was his brother, Warren, who was to prove a close and lifelong friend. The great annual event was the month at the seashore, a season that set Lewis's father glumly fidgeting, for he was a man of routine and did not adapt easily to the idleness of vacation time.

In 1905 came the move to the "New House" —Little Lea. It was at the ultimate edge of suburbia, close to open farmland. The house itself will be recognized by any reader of the *Narnia* stories. There were all sorts of odd bits of space for children to explore. In particular, the top floor, where the two boys lived their intensely private lives, was full of huge dark areas connected by mysterious tunnels.

It was shortly before the move to the New House that young Clive announced to his family his change of name. Henceforth he was to be Jacksie. He refused to answer to any other name. Progressively shortened to Jacks and then Jack, it remained his first name throughout his life. At Oxford, depending on the degree of familiarity, he was Mr. (or Dr.) Lewis, Lewis, or Jack.

The two boys spent many unsupervised hours on the mysterious top floor, creating a world of their own imagination. Lewis had a particular passion for talking animals, and eagerly read the early Beatrix Potter stories. But when he came to write his own animal stories (beginning at the age of five and continuing until his early teens) he created a curiously prosaic animal land, "Boxen." The tales show little of the magic and mystery that make the *Narnia* stories so luminous. In fact, Jack's talking animals seemed to spend most of their time —as did the men that Lewis's father knew—in discussing politics. (The relatively small role that politics plays in Lewis's adult books may well reflect the eventual nausea of the small boy, forced to listen to countless political diatribes at the dinner table.)

Always, visible on the far horizon stood a line of high blue hills beyond easy exploration, but replete with lure and invitation. They haunted Lewis and reappear in *The Pilgrim's Regress,* where they symbolize the unknown, the numinous—what he called "Joy" or "Romance."

Paradise came to an end. When Lewis was nine, his mother died of cancer. Soon thereafter there began his adventures in a succession of boarding schools. For the most part he detested them so fiercely that this antipathy later spills over into the books he wrote in adulthood.

One of the schools, called Belsen in *Surprised by Joy,* had for its headmaster a man who was later certified as insane. At another school he had some good instruction, but was out of sympathy with the rough and sometimes sadistic practices of the students. As he reported later, the most humane aspect of the school was the widespread homosexuality, which at least involved some kindness and affection. Bored by the daily routine of the school and antagonistic to its customs, Lewis wrote to his father and asked to be sent elsewhere. His father consented, and made arrangements for him to become a pupil of W. T. Kirkpatrick, at Great Bookham in Surrey. This proved a perfect solution, and a turning point in Lewis's intellectual development.

Kirkpatrick was like a character out of a Scottish novel. Dour and warmhearted both, he was a merciless logician, eradicating through the dialectic process any fuzziness and nonsense in his pupil's head. He was also a rationalist atheist of the stern and highly moral 19th century variety, and thus a comfort and support to young Lewis, who by now had lost what shreds of Christian belief he had once possessed. Anyone who wishes to meet the "Great Knock" and observe him in action will find him lovingly portrayed under the alias of MacPhee in *That Hideous Strength.*

At this point something should be said about Lewis's loss of religious faith. The faith was not too strong from the beginning. The family adhered to the Anglican Church, but without much passion or zeal. The doubts began as early as his mother's death from cancer. He could not reconcile her suffering with what he had been taught about a God who was completely good and could do anything He chose to do. Another important factor in his retreat from Christianity was the matron at one of his schools. She was intensely interested in spiritualism and theosophy. Though he did not formally adopt any of her ideas, he was intrigued by them. Here was someone whom he admired, but who held beliefs quite different from those of his family. He concluded that "truth" is a vague and hazy thing, not to be identified with any particular and precise set of beliefs.

This relativistic way of regarding religion was intensified when he studied the Greek and Latin classics. He noted that the scholars took for granted the human origin of the ancient deities. He asked himself whether there was any good reason to attribute Zeus to human imagination while insisting that Jehovah was objectively real. By the time Lewis came under Kirkpatrick's influence he was already a convinced atheist. The irony was that the very habits of rigorous thought that the sturdy old atheist taught him were in time to prove one of the two roads back to the faith that he had rejected.

Kirkpatrick early recognized Lewis's scholarly and creative ability, and informed Mr. Lewis that he must reckon with all that these gifts involve. Meanwhile, the stay at Great Bookham was more than a Platonic symposium. Its practical purpose was to coach Lewis for Oxford in the hope that he could win a scholarship. Brilliant as he was, he was not an automatic winner, and indeed the next few years of his life included many apparent failures and disappointments. The first one was when he did not receive a classical scholarship at New College, Oxford. The blow was sweetened when he did win one at University.

His studies were soon interrupted by World War I. Not a pacifist by conviction, though at the same time not personally attracted to the military life, he decided to join the O.T.C., and in due course was commissioned a second lieutenant. Meanwhile, he had failed the mathematics component of a required examination, and was faced by the prospect that never, no matter how well coached he might be, could he hope to pass the most elementary test in mathematics. By an irony of history, the war saved him, since those who served were eventually exempt from the examination.

Lewis's reasonably affirmative attitude toward military service (later in his books he was to argue against the pacifist position) may owe something to his brother, Warnie, who was already in uniform and became a career soldier, rising to the rank of major. Lewis's own career was brief and mildly comic. In his memoirs he pays tribute to the experienced and tactful sergeant who told him what orders to issue, and he admits he did not have the military temperament. Still, he served on the front line during late 1917 and early 1918 when the Germans were making their final, desperate assault. A British shell landed short of its target, and wounded him from the rear, a subject about which Lewis was wont to jest. He was hospitalized and shifted from one convalescent camp to another. The war dragged to an end; Lewis was demobilized in December 1918, and next month found himself back at Oxford, a student again.

During his training as an army officer Lewis struck up a warm friendship with E. F. C. ("Paddy") Moore, and became acquainted with Paddy's mother. Apparently Lewis promised Paddy to look after his mother if need be. Paddy was killed in the War, and a couple of years later, Lewis, Mrs. Moore, and her daughter set up combined lodgings. For thirty years he was a kind of son to a kind of mother. This relation puzzled and sometimes irritated Warnie and Lewis's friends. In time, the situation became a major complication in his life, but it seems to have begun with high and idealist hopes on both sides.

At Oxford Lewis's brilliance was widely recognized, but much of the competition was brilliant also. At times he sank into despair. Off and on he was driven to grade high school examinations in order to earn a little money. He was lucky in his father, who believed in him, and provided enough basic support so that Lewis could continue his studies and job hunting.

In 1924 a break came. E. F. Carritt was invited to spend a year lecturing at the University of Michigan. Lewis took his place for the year, as tutor in philosophy. By the end of that year a more promising opening came. He was elected tutor in English Language and Literature at Magdalen College. He continued in this position until he received a Cambridge professorship in 1954.

Meanwhile and for a long time, his ambition was to be a poet. As early as 1919 he published *Spirits in Bondage,* which disappeared almost without trace in the great floodtide of "modern poetry." Lewis as a poet was definitely not modern; his kinship was more with the great epic and narrative poets of the past. Perhaps he lived in the wrong epoch for the particular talent he had. He was very much out of joint with the poetic times, and it was years—if ever—before he could see any validity in such poetry as T. S. Eliot's.

For many years Lewis had had in mind an extended philosophic-narrative poem, *Dymer,* which he finally completed and published in 1926. It received some respectful reviews but again seemed so much out of the poetic mainstream that it left little mark. Lewis apparently grew discouraged, and turned mainly to prose, though he did publish an occasional poem in periodicals. I suspect, though without proof, that he esteemed his prose less and his poetry more than most of his readers do. Certainly, it is as a prose writer that Lewis became and remains famous.

From 1924 to 1954 Lewis was simply another don at Oxford. Like the others, he took his pupils one or two at a time, from 10:00 to 1:00 and again from 5:00 to 7:00. They would bring their weekly essays with them, read them aloud, and receive his trenchant comments.

In the fragments of time left over, Lewis prepared his lectures, did his writing, and—after he became famous—handled as best he could a fantastic load of correspondence. His literary productivity during the thirty years as an Oxford don is staggering, all the more so when one takes into account the combined household and Mrs. Moore's habit of using him for domestic chores as though he were an extra maid. He was as short of money as of time in these early days, for he had to stretch a salary intended for a bachelor to cover the needs of his "family."

The legends of Lewis's male chauvinism abound. And there is some documentation. In an autobiographical sketch he was guilty of admitting, "There's no sound I like better than adult male laughter." One biographical directory even asserted that he frequently locked himself into his room when female figures appeared at the college. I sent Lewis this write-up and he bluntly replied:

" . . . pure bosh. For one thing women are wandering through the 'college precincts' the whole blessed day. For another, having taken female pupils of all ages, shapes, sizes, and complexions for about twenty years, I am a bit tougher than the story makes out. If I ever have fled from a female visitor it was not because she was a woman but because she was a *bore*, or because she was the fifteenth visitor on a busy day."

In *Surprised by Joy* Lewis later hinted cryptically at affairs he had in his youth. But once he was in full stride at Oxford, carrying on the work of a tutor and becoming established as a writer, he was in what was still very much a man's world. This seems not to have troubled him.

The real mystery is his relation with Mrs. Moore, a woman who seems to have been lacking in charm of any variety. Lewis's brother, who admittedly despised the lady, describes her thus:[2]

> She was a woman of very limited mind, and notably domineering and possessive by temperament. She cut down to a minimum his visits to his father, interfered constantly with his work, and imposed upon him a heavy burden of minor domestic tasks. In twenty years I never saw a book in her hands; her conversation was chiefly about herself, and was otherwise a matter of ill-informed dogmatism: her mind was of a type that he found barely tolerable elsewhere.

In fairness to Mrs. Moore, she also served as a convenient excuse when Lewis was invited to do something he really didn't want to do, such as go on a lecture trip to America. Strange as the relationship seemed to those who knew

2. W. H. Lewis, ed., *Letters of C. S. Lewis* (New York: Harcourt Brace World, 1966), p. 12.

Lewis, it continued until 1948 when Mrs. Moore, her mind almost gone, had to be put in a nursing home. Lewis visited her every day until her death in 1951. By that time, the stage was almost set for him to meet his future wife, Joy Davidman Gresham.

¶

In his late twenties, Lewis had been slowly moving back toward theism and finally Christianity. Part of the process was, ironically, the gift of the good atheist, Kirkpatrick. The Scotsman had trained Lewis's mind to smell nonsense and fallacies and to destroy them by a merciless dialectic process. Soon Lewis found himself testing these weapons against various philosophic stances—popular realism, philosophical idealism, pantheism—and discovering deeper logical flaws in these systems then in theism. Theism itself, which stood up well under logical scrutiny, proved for Lewis the anteroom of Christianity. All this is spelled out fully in *Surprised by Joy,* and presented more schematically in *Mere Christianity.*

The other path leading finally back to Christianity is what Lewis called "Joy" or "Romance." This refers to the fleeting experience almost everyone· probably has at one time or another. It may be triggered by a bar of music, a landscape, a forgotten memory. The experience is an instantaneous sense of seeing into the heart of things, as though a universe beyond the universe opened itself wide for an instant and as instantly slammed its doors shut. It is an experience the Romantic poets, such as Wordsworth, often describe, and it has parallels with some kinds of religious mysticism. In *Surprised by Joy* the guerrilla raids by "Joy" are described, and their role in his eventual if reluctant acceptance of Christianity is sketched.

The first experience of "Joy" was in Lewis's early boyhood, after the family had moved to the new and mysterious house. He was standing beside a flowering currant bush when—[3]

... there suddenly arose in me without warning, as if from a depth not of years but of centuries, the memory of that earlier morning at the Old House when my brother had brought his toy garden into the nursery. It is

3. *Surprised by Joy*, p. 16.

difficult to find words strong enough for the sensation which came over me; Milton's "enormous bliss" of Eden . . . comes somewhere near it. It was a sensation, of course, of desire; but desire for what? Not, certainly, for a biscuit tin filled with moss, nor even (though that came into it) for my own past.

The moment passed quickly away; the ecstasy and the desire vanished; the world turned commonplace.

A second experience of "Joy" came through a Beatrix Potter book, *Squirrel Nutkin,* from which he mysteriously perceived "the Idea of Autumn" and had the same sense of sudden, unplanned revelation that the memory of the toy garden had given him.

A third boyhood experience was produced by reading Longfellow's *Saga of King Olaf.* When he came to the lines[4] "I heard a voice that cried, ⁄ Balder the beautiful ⁄ Is dead, is dead—" the effect was overpowering:

I knew nothing about Balder; but instantly I was uplifted into huge regions of northern sky, I desired with almost sickening inten⁄

4. *Surprised by Joy.*

sity something never to be described (except that it is cold, spacious, severe, pale, and remote) and then, as in the other examples, found myself at the very same moment already falling out of that desire and wishing I were back in it.

For long stretches of time Lewis would remain unvisited by any intimation of "Joy," then it would come unannounced and in full strength. While he was in boarding school he picked up a magazine and came on a reference to *Siegfried and the Twilight of the Gods*. Immediately the earlier vision of pure Northernness engulfed him. So the fleeting revelations continued off and on through the years. They were *not,* Lewis insisted with absolute conviction, a sexual sublimation. He was to find in early manhood that sexual pleasure did not banish, neutralize, or replace the vision of some kind of delight that comes from outside three-dimensional space.

At the age of seventeen, Lewis by chance picked up a copy of *Phantastes,* a novel by the 19th century Scottish minister and writer, George MacDonald. He found the book somehow akin to the mysterious revelations he had encountered in moments of "Joy." Years later, when he went on an imaginary trip through the other world in *The Great Divorce,* it was George MacDonald who served as his guide. Writing of *Phantastes,* Lewis said: "That night my imagination was, in a certain sense, baptized; the rest of me, not unnaturally, took longer. I had not the faintest notion what I had let myself in for by buying *Phantastes*."[5]

There were, then, two converging roads that led Lewis back to the religion he had so happily renounced. One was the workings of his mind, particularly as he tried to make sense of the odd fact that mankind seems, with minor cultural variations, to have a sense of a universal, objective moral law, while frantically disobeying the demands of that law. The other road was the way of "Romance" or "Joy," the experience of a yearning whose object was unknown; the intimation of a dimension of reality that common sense and finely honed reason were equally incapable of explaining. By the

5. *Surprised by Joy.*

age of thirty he glumly felt God closing in on him.:[6]

> You must picture me alone in that room in Magdalen, night after night, feeling, whenever my mind lifted even for a second from my work, the steady, unrelenting approach of Him whom I so earnestly desired not to meet. That which I greatly feared had at last come upon me. In the Trinity Term of 1929 I gave in, and admitted that God was God, and knelt and prayed: perhaps, that night, the most dejected and reluctant convert in all England.

For a few months more, he was undecided about the role of Christ. He wrestled with the New Testament, haunted by its central figure, and finally found himself convinced that one time and one time only the old myths of a God descending to earth had become historical fact; that the Jesus so sharply outlined in the New Testament was one with the God who had captured a reluctant convert during Trinity Term.

Lewis's conversion provided the impetus for

6. *Surprised by Joy.*

a very large part of his subsequent writing. The particular route he traveled, from mild faith to atheism and back (or on) to strong faith, also helped make him sympathetic to nonbelievers, since he knew their problems firsthand.

The first book resulting from his conversion was a tale modeled on Bunyan, *The Pilgrim's Regress* (1933). Written rather heavily, and sometimes unpleasantly sharp-edged (as Lewis recognized later), *The Pilgrim's Regress* has never attracted wide attention. But for anyone curious about Lewis's life and opinions, and most of all about the factors leading him back to the Christian faith, the book is fascinating. The subtitle, "An Allegorical Apology for Christianity, Reason, and Romanticism," suggests the central theme, the quest for a way of looking at experience that will satisfy both the mind and the heart.

The tale concerns John, a boy born in Puritania, who learns at an early age that a mysterious Landlord owns everything and forbids him to do many pleasant things. Simultaneously he has strange experiences of "Joy"—upon gazing into a woodland not far from his home he hears enchanting music and catches a glimpse of a tranquil sea and an island. He experiences such intense yearning that he embarks on a lifelong pilgrimage to find the island.

Along the way John meets various allegorical helpers or enemies. The pilgrimage is long and arduous, but all ends well. John explores both false and half-true answers to his questions, and with the help of Mother Kirk (the Church) learns at last that the Landlord *is* real but different from the tyrant of his boyhood fears. The island is also real and can be reached, though only if one follows the correct directions.

Up to this point in Lewis's life—his mid-thirties—he had a marginal reputation as a poet, had attracted some modest attention as a religious writer, but so far had not produced a major work of literary scholarship. Anyone who had known him at Oxford during this period of his life would have remembered him as one don among many, but an unusually effective lecturer, and very bright. Such an observer might have wondered when this obviously superior mind was to produce a book worthy of its potential.

For some years, Lewis had been playing around with a cluster of ideas—the allegory as a literary form, various concepts of love, the changing relation through time between love and marriage. The result was finally *The Allegory of Love* (1936), a book that received important academic honors and immediately won for Lewis a respected niche in the world of scholarship. This, in fact, is the book often mentioned by those who deplore the later diversion of his energies to religious writing—"If only Lewis had followed up *The Allegory* with other equally important books in literary history, instead of *that other stuff!*" as one Oxford scholar put it to me.

The Allegory of Love is a marvelously readable book, even for anyone who is no specialist in the subject. By the time he composed this work, Lewis's prose style had matured to the ease, grace, and wit that his readers came to expect. He was moving toward the sureness and facility that made it sometimes possible for him to write out a new book in longhand, make a few changes between lines and in the margins, and then turn it over to a typist for the final manuscript.

The Allegory of Love deals with two closely intertwined subjects. One is the evolution of the allegory as a literary form from Greco-Roman times to the Elizabethan period. The other is the strange history of courtly love, which began in southern France during the early Middle Ages. This highly stylized expression of passion typically involved a young man and a somewhat older and married lady. The forms of the amorous ritual were infinitely refined, and the lady was safe on her pedestal as long as she chose to remain there, but the ultimate goal of the game was physical union—and strict secrecy, of course. It was a system of man-woman relationship in rivalry with the stern Christian insistence on complete chastity outside of marriage. The book traces the gradual process by which the ideal of courtly love gradually merges with the concept of marriage, so that by the time of Spenser's *Fairie Queene* the newest novelty is romantic marriage. The literary and cultural strands of the book come together as Lewis considers the ways in which the allegorical form was used to express changing patterns of love.

I suppose one could turn psychoanalyst at this point, and meditate upon Lewis's relation with an older woman, Mrs. Moore. The pictures of her gleaned from the testimony of his friends do not sound much like the heroines of courtly romance, but then the witnesses were not inclined to give her the benefit of any doubts. Perhaps Lewis felt more at ease in a relationship where marriage was not a lively threat. If one must be psychoanalytic, some concept of mother substitute (his own mother died early) seems more likely.

Looking ahead, the reader of *The Allegory of Love* might ask himself whether it throws any light on the eventual relation, culminating in marriage, between Lewis and Joy Davidman Gresham. I doubt it. Joy was not the sort of woman to be typecast as a heroine of courtly romances. She was too direct—even "masculine," some might say, meaning that she had plenty of brains in her head, and did not hesitate to use them in debate with a sweetheart, husband, or anyone else. Again using sexist language, there was something "man to man" in the pleasure that Lewis and Joy were to take in each other, as well as an intense delight in the fact that when God undertook the task of creation and invented the human race, "male and female created he them." Joy was not a Mrs. Moore, nor an ultrarefined and reticent lady installed on an unapproachable pedestal. She was a magnificent and complete human being, one capable of intense love, and response to the love that she inspired.

Throughout his writing career, Lewis alternated his works of scholarship with title after title of imaginative and religious writing. *A Preface to "Paradise Lost"* (1942) remains a sturdily useful introduction to Milton, and is one of the best refutations of the Romantic theory that Satan is really the hero of the epic. *English Literature in the Sixteenth Century, Excluding Drama* (Volume III of what Lewis called "Oh Hell"—*The Oxford History of English Literature*) appeared in 1954 and was widely hailed as a brilliantly fresh look at the writers of that period. Among his other scholarly works, the posthumously published *Discarded Image* is particularly useful, with its clear presentation of the Medieval worldview.

I suppose every admirer of Lewis has his favorite date as the starting point for his full literary maturity. I would have to list two dates. The first is 1936 for *The Allegory of Love*. The other is 1938 when *Out of the Silent Planet* was published. In this book, the first of a space-exploration trilogy, the soaring imagination of Lewis and his Christian sensibility come together in a tale where space itself seems baptized and radiant with the presence of the divine.

The plot itself is slight enough. The hero, a philologist significantly named Ransom, is seized by Devine (a gold prospector) and Weston (a half-mad scientist who wishes humanity to colonize the universe). Ransom is taken by spaceship to Mars. His captors are planning to offer him to the Martians as a sacrifice for their gods, but it turns out that the beings on the planet are benevolent. In fact, they worship the same God as Ransom. The difference is that Adam and Eve fell through disobedience and were expelled from paradise; there has been no loss of innocence on Mars.

Ransom escapes and wanders through the astonishingly vivid landscape. Finally he is summoned to the court of Oyarsa, the presiding archangel of the planet. Weston and Devine are on trial for killing a Martian. Oyarsa decides they are incapable of knowing right from wrong, and orders them back to the earth. Ransom is offered a chance to stay on a planet where all is divine harmony, but decides to join his companions and return to old Thulcandra, "the silent planet." (The earth is silent because God has quarantined it and cut it off from communication with the other planets, to prevent the spread of corruption.)

A few years later Lewis completed the trilogy. The second volume, *Perelandra* (1943), has Ransom on Venus, a planet of paradisaic floating islands, where the Adam and Eve of that world have been freshly created, and no serpent has corrupted their innocence. The whole book is aglow with mythological beauty, so real to the reader that Perelandra lingers in his memory like a country he once visited, or hopes to visit in some impossible future. This may not be the greatest of Lewis's books, but it is the one that most haunts me, and that impelled me to write to Lewis, feeling in my heart that we shared a vision of what the universe is all about.

The concluding volume of the trilogy is *That Hideous Strength* (1945), an apocalyptic novel almost too full of supernatural fury. The center of the action is the National Institute of Co-ordinated Experiments, a front for demonic powers trying to take possession of the earth. The sleeping Merlin is drawn into the struggle, there are echoes of the Tower of Babel story, a young sociologist and his wife—both modern rationalists—find themselves caught in the crossfire of good and evil. All ends well, though the reader is shellshocked by the time he reaches the last page. The book lacks the beauty and mythic depth of the two earlier ones, but succeeds in making the forces of good and evil overwhelmingly real.

In 1940, Lewis published his first book dealing with a specific theological dilemma, *The*

Problem of Pain. He wrote it at the suggestion of a publisher who was bringing out a "Christian Challenge" series dealing in popular style with aspects of the Christian religion. The work was a success, eventually selling more than 120,000 copies in England alone, and establishing the author as someone who could speak to the ordinary lay audience. It did not, however, escape some sharp criticisms from readers who found the whole work a little too pat. All in all, perhaps the book treats the intractable problem of pain about as adequately as anyone, attempting to make religious sense of it, has been able to do. Ultimately all attempts end in a degree of patness or a confession of ignorance. Lewis was to learn this when years in the future his wife lay dying of cancer.

The stage was now set for Lewis's enormous popularity as a religious writer, and the sudden leap of his fame across the Atlantic. Soon he was receiving an appalling number of letters from American readers, warning him that the Devil was mad at him, or proposing matrimony, or raising some theological question, or asking pastoral advice about some personal problem.

The turning point was *The Screwtape Letters,* first serialized in a religious periodical, and then published in book form (1942). The idea suddenly came to Lewis as he was leaving church one Sunday—dramatize the psychology of temptation from the Enemy's viewpoint. The form he chose was a series of letters from Screwtape, an experienced tempter in the Infernal Civil Service, to his young nephew, Wormwood, who is endeavoring to bring about the spiritual downfall of a young man recently converted to Christianity. Wormwood is a romantic, dreaming about some spectacular success. His uncle advises him that quiet sins can be equally deadly, and it is only the final damnation that counts in the eyes of Hell's lords. What the book achieves is a very detailed and subtle study of a normal young Christian, caught between the demands and promises of his new found faith, and all the ideas and temptations working to destroy it.

The book was immensely successful, in sales

and in critical reactions. From this moment Lewis was "typed" as an incisive, witty, and stubbornly orthodox defender of historical Christianity—a latterday G. K. Chesterton. The fame and acclaim he earned through *The Screwtape Letters* proved an irritation to Lewis. He had not enjoyed writing the book; there were many others he had written that he valued more highly.

Meanwhile, Lewis was speaking on religious matters at RAF bases and drawing groups of varying size and response. More importantly, he became a radio celebrity. Invited to give a series of four talks in 1941, he was soon a household word. During the next few years he delivered several additional series of talks. A revised version of his various radio lectures was published in the form of three slender volumes. Later he again revised these and combined them into one book, *Mere Christianity* (1952). Because of its compression, this work necessarily oversimplifies some knotty questions, but it has the virtues of clarity and effective exposition, and has rivaled *The Screwtape Letters* in its sales. For a brief introduction to the doctrines of historic Christianity, this book is a good place to begin.

Lewis's leap to fame coincides with the period of World War II. The cynical may suggest a causal link. At a time when the visible world presents few cheering sights, men are driven to supernatural hopes and consolations. There may be a germ of truth in this, since a widespread interest in religion emerged during the early 1940s and continued into the early 1950s. But it is equally true that Lewis was just reaching the point in his own development as a thinker and writer where he could make effective contact with an ordinary reading or listening public.

Lewis's life was simple and orderly in the 1940s, when he first became well known. In addition to his rooms at Magdalen College, where he often stayed overnight, he owned the rambling brick house, The Kilns, on the outskirts of Oxford, where Mrs. Moore was installed. He received his pupils in his Oxford rooms, and indeed few people seem ever to have set foot inside The Kilns during the time Mrs. Moore was resident. I recall his apologizing for not inviting me to his home during my first trip to England. He explained that his "mother" was in ill health, if I remember correctly.

Lewis's popular reputation did not lead to any official recognition by Oxford University. By a kind of academic snobbery, the enormous BBC audiences and vast readership of *The Screwtape Letters* probably diminished his chances of a professorship which would have freed much more time for writing. His ardent espousal of Christianity was not calculated to win promotion, and even those colleagues who did not object to his religion often wished he would concentrate more on English scholarship, which after all was supposed to be his specialty. So, as long as he remained at Oxford, he was still forced to meet his daily quota of pupils and struggle for the occasional hour during which he could write the books that were steadily increasing his international fame.

Lewis was not gregarious, but he had a warm gift of friendship, which he exercised with comparatively few of the people whose lives intersected with his. A friendship once formed usually lasted. One principal way he kept in touch with friends was the Inklings. The little group began in the 1930s and continued until 1950. The membership fluctuated somewhat over the years and would sometimes include visitors. They would meet Thursday evenings in Lewis's rooms at Magdalen, and read aloud the writing they were doing. This was followed by frank discussion and criticism. The group included Lewis's brother (who became a well-known scholar in the field of French History), J. R. R. Tolkien, Nevill Coghill, Owen Barfield, and Charles Williams. The latter was an amazing, largely self-taught Cockney, remembered especially for his seven novels in which the natural and supernatural interact on human affairs. He was reading aloud, to the group, the chapters of one of these, *All Hallows' Eve,* during the same period that Lewis was reading from the rough draft of *Perelandra.*

An overlapping group met in the late morning almost every Tuesday at a pub officially named the Eagle and Child but always called the Bird and Baby. By tradition but no formal arrangement the back room was theirs. This was more an occasion for witty and sometimes profound conversation, and for the simple pleasure of renewing long time friendships. These meetings continued to the end of Lewis's life.

Though not given to formal sports, Lewis was a vigorous man, fond of the out-of-doors. He especially enjoyed long hiking trips, though insisting that they be planned so as to arrive at a good place for high tea in the late afternoon. He and Warnie explored many of the rural parts of England and Ireland, and were often joined by a few close friends.

Meanwhile, Lewis was developing a world-wide network of relationships, some of which could be called long distance friendships, as a result of his books. Total strangers would write to him, asking complicated personal or theological questions. Lewis tried to answer as many letters as possible between breakfast and the arrival of the first pupil of the day. No one knows how many of his handwritten replies lie scattered throughout the world. In effect, he became a kind of pastoral counselor. Frequently his brother, who had more or less mastered the art of typing, would assist him.

All through the forties and early fifties the flood of his books continued. I shall mention only a few. *The Abolition of Man* (1943) is a brilliant attack on all philosophies that explain away the moral sense. *The Great Divorce* (1946), with its picture of the gray city that is purgatory for those who accept the invitation to transfer to heaven, and hell for those who insist on remaining, is the nearest modern equivalent to Dante's *Divine Comedy*. *Miracles* (1947) deals with one specific theological problem, and with more success than *The Problem of Pain*. Most important, the first of the seven *Narnia* tales, to prove equally popular with children and adults, appeared under the title of *The Lion, the Witch and the Wardrobe*. At the rate of about one a year, the others followed to nourish a hungry market of readers: *Prince Caspian, The Voyage of the "Dawn Treader," The Silver Chair, The Horse and His Boy, The Magician's Nephew,* and *The Last Battle*.

In 1955 Lewis's long awaited spiritual autobiography, *Surprised by Joy*, appeared. It is deliberately reticent about the mundane personal experiences that are the substance of most autobiographies, but very full in its revelation of the events and insights that led him from atheism to theism and eventually to traditional Christianity. Here the reader learns in detail of early childhood influences, the impact of schools and books, most of all the impact of the "Great Knock." Traced parallel with the intellectual odyssey is the more mysterious experience of "Joy" or "Romance," the sudden moments of insight and revelation that led him in the same direction that his questioning mind, sharpened by the Scotsman's dialectic, finally chose. Much about Lewis's long drawn out conversion experience that was merely hinted at or described obliquely in earlier books, is presented with power and naked directness in *Surprised by Joy*.

In 1954 Lewis finally became a professor, but not at Oxford. The invitation came from the rival university, Cambridge. In his inaugural address he referred to himself as a dinosaur, or "Old Western man." He argued that paganism and Christianity shared more in common than either shares with a secularized modern world. His new position at Cambridge gave him more time for writing, but did not result in a radical change in his habits. The house on the outskirts of Oxford continued to be his home, and he spent as many long weekends there as possible, commuting to Cambridge by train.

¶

It is now necessary to backtrack a few years to record the intersection of Lewis's life with that of Joy Davidman Gresham, the woman he eventually married. Here an odd coincidence almost makes one believe that life imitates art, even to the extent of enjoying a good pun. The title of Lewis's autobiography was *not* inspired by his acquaintance with Joy Davidman Gresham. He had already selected the title—a phrase from Wordsworth—before she figured significantly in his life. But by chance the title did become doubly appropriate, and Lewis's friends were not above remarking that he had been "surprised by Joy"—which, like most

good puns, is at least a partial truth. I am sure
marriage was not in his mind when he first met
her, still less lurking in his fantasies some years
earlier when she, in the midst of her own conversion experience, had come on his books,
found them exciting and helpful, and in her
forthright way struck up a fan letter correspondence with the confirmed bachelor don.

By another odd coincidence, Joy and her
husband, William Lindsay Gresham, had
been close friends of my wife and me for some
years before Joy and Lewis met, though meanwhile she had initiated a vigorous correspondence with him. Joy, sixteen years Lewis's
junior, came of a secularized Jewish background in New York City. She was for a time
a member of the Communist Party, and her
book of proletarian verse, *Letter to a Comrade,*
won the Yale Series of Younger Poets Award
for 1938. Later she published more poetry and
several promising novels. She was not a beautiful woman except for her eyes, which were
large, dark, lustrous, and bright with probing
intelligence. She had a particular knack for

wielding the sword of her wit to cut away intellectual nonsense; in the thrust and parry of debate she was a match for Lewis.

Joy's husband, Bill, was of gentile background. He, too, was for a time a Communist and served on the Loyalist side in the Spanish civil war. He was a gifted novelist, and one of his books, *Nightmare Alley,* was made into a film. A great raconteur with a folk sense of humor, he had the charm of a bright and somewhat impish boy of fourteen. It eventually became clear that he was a good deal of a spoiled boy, and that his psychological maturity was at about the fourteen-year-old level. But he did have charm and warmth, and I remember him fondly.

Bill and Joy had two small boys. When I first met them, theirs seemed an ideal marriage. They had both experienced a gradual religious conversion and were committed Christians by this time. Their professional futures seemed bright. They lived in a mansion they had purchased from the movie rights to Bill's novel. (They had previously been so poor they had not been paying an income tax, and when they finally hit it rich, in their innocence they failed to set aside money for the IRS. The latter put a lien on the big house.)

As I came to know them better, I could sense tensions and stresses, Bill's roving eye being one of the factors. Gradually the strains accumulated. Finally, in 1952 Joy took the two boys, then eight and seven, with her on a trip to England to get away from a depressing domestic situation and try to see her life in perspective. Whether she had any romantic fantasies in mind about Lewis—who knows? If she did, she kept them to herself.

Joy and Lewis at last met. A warm friendship, based in part on strong and mutual respect, began to flower. In time, according to the Green-Hooper biography, Lewis felt that things were moving too fast and put the brakes on. Meanwhile, word reached Joy that Bill was in love with a woman back home. Joy returned to the States, declined his invitation to set up a *ménage à trois,* and agreed to a divorce, with the custody of the boys given to her. In 1954 she and the boys were back in England. It was a year or so later that my wife and I visited in

England and had a chance to observe Joy and
Lewis together. She seemed to be at The Kilns
a good deal. My wife firmly declared, "I smell
marriage in the air." Whether Lewis smelled it
is more doubtful.

After some months Joy's health began to fail.
The diagnosis at first was acute rheumatism.
Early in 1957 it was clearly cancer. Other
problems were multiplying. Toward the beginning of 1956 the Home Office, giving no
reasons, refused to renew Joy's residence permit. Lewis came to the rescue (as in the 1930s
W. H. Auden rescued Thomas Mann's daughter from deportation). On April 23, 1956,
Lewis and Joy were married at the Oxford
registry office, thus giving her and the two boys
British nationality.

Two days later Lewis explained to Green
that this was purely a practical formality and
had nothing to do with real marriage. Joy was
now safe from deportation, but her health began to fail rapidly, and the verdict of cancer
seemed to seal her destiny. She did not want to
die in a hospital, and Lewis felt he could not
bring her to live in The Kilns unless they were

religiously married. He found a minister will-
ing to solemnize the marriage of a divorced
person, and the ceremony was held in the hospital. It was assumed that the bride had little
time left to live; the cancer had already eaten
through her thigh bone.

After Joy was installed at The Kilns, a hopeless invalid, the expert on miracles experienced
one before his own eyes. A remission occurred.
Joy wrote us in mid-1957:

> My case is definitely arrested for the time be-
> ing—I may be alright for three or four years.
> There's a faint hope [the bone] may knit
> enough to let me hobble around a little in a
> caliper . . . . Jack and I are managing to be
> surprisingly happy considering the circum-
> stances; you'd think we were a honeymoon
> couple in our early twenties, rather than our
> middle-aged selves.

By slow degrees Joy moved from bed to wheel-
chair to cane to almost normal walking, except
that the cancerous leg was now shorter than the
other. As her recovery progressed, we received
other letters in which she bubbled over with
happiness (if one can use such language of a

person who had her austere side) and cele-
brated Lewis's prowess as a lover. The marriage that began *pro forma* became very much
the real thing as soon as she was physically
recovered.

By his marriage Lewis had become, in effect,
the father of two boys, and had acquired a wife
who had the practical common sense that he
often lacked. He was an incredibly unworldly
person about such things as money. Once he
became famous and had a lot of it, he gave
most of it away through a charitable founda-
tion he established. The rest he put into a
checking account. He had never heard of sav-
ings accounts. Joy had, and took care of the
transfer in short order. Lewis had also been
plagued by hordes of teddy boys and their girl
friends who invaded the wood lot attached to
their property. Joy solved this problem simply,
by patrolling the woods with a gun. I remember when our children went into the woods to
play, a boy from the neighborhood ran up and
called out to them that they'd better leave "or
Mrs. Lewis will shoot you."

If these capitalistic attitudes seem odd in one

who had once been a Communist, the story is the familiar one of the radical gradually turning conservative. By the end of her life, she was a staunch advocate of the noose and the birch, and could direct a withering fire of destructive criticism against conventional academic liberalism. Meanwhile, she flowered as a woman —and a human being. It was, I think, an extraordinarily happy and buoyant marriage, though the shadow hovered always in the background.

During the years they were together, Lewis wrote several books which clearly reflect the influence Joy had upon his writing. One was Lewis's most profound novel, though far from his most popular, *Till We Have Faces,* written in 1956.

This is a retelling of the Cupid and Psyche legend, which had haunted him for more than thirty years. In his version, Psyche's older sister, Orual, is the principal character. Orual is plain, as Joy was plain, but like Joy capable of intense Philia as well as Eros. Her life involves a religious quest that leads at last to the one God; here there is a clear parallel to Joy's progression from atheistic Communism to Christianity. These are only the most obvious resemblances. Anyone knowing Joy would recognize many of her other traits in Orual, who is beyond question the most profoundly developed female character in Lewis's books. I would go further and say that in this book Lewis achieved a depth of human insight that excelled anything else he wrote, and pointed toward a talent for fiction that might have put him with the major novelists, if time and health had permitted him to continue.

The Four Loves was originally written as four lectures for broadcast in America under religious auspices. In revised form it was published in 1960. It is thematically closely akin to *Till We Have Faces* since it analyzes four kinds of love—Affection, Friendship, Eros, and Charity. Lewis himself had experienced Affection in an exaggerated form with Mrs. Moore; he had good, abiding friends and through them knew Friendship; he had sought to practice the spiritual love that is called Charity. Eros he had experienced in his youth, then during the

long years of his bachelorhood he had turned
away from it, even avoiding foods that he found
sexually stimulating. Then along came Joy.
The course of events gave him first-hand experience of what sexual love between a man
and woman can be at its best.

This new understanding infuses *The Four
Loves*. In his earlier books, such as *Mere Christianity*, Lewis had concentrated on the legalities
of sexual love—confine it to marriage, otherwise be chaste. He also informed Christians
that divorce was out as far as they were concerned. Now, married to a divorced woman
and feeling his marriage amply blessed, Lewis
writes as one who has the authority of experience, and not as some remote observer. This is
particularly evident when he discusses the
comic aspects of sexual love:[7]

She herself [Venus] is a mocking, mis-
chievous spirit, far more elf than deity, and
makes game of us. When all external cir-
cumstances are fittest for her service she will

7. C. S. Lewis, *The Four Loves* (New York: Harcourt
Brace World, 1960).

leave one or both of the lovers totally indisposed for it. When every overt act is impossible and even glances cannot be exchanged—in trains, in shops, and at interminable parties—she will assail them with all her force. An hour later, when time and place agree, she will have mysteriously withdrawn; perhaps from only one of them. What a pother this must raise—what resentments, self-pities, suspicions, wounded vanities and all the current chatter about "frustration"—in those who have deified her! But sensible lovers laugh. It is all part of the game; a game of catch-as-catch-can, and the escapes and tumbles and head-on collisions are to be treated as a romp.

In August 1958 we find Lewis writing to a friend:[8] "We had a holiday—you might call it a belated honeymoon—in Ireland and were lucky enough to get that perfect fortnight in July." He went on to describe the beautifully sensuous landscape, and to recount the first experience either had had traveling by air.

"I never expected to have, in my sixties, the

8. Robert Lancelyn Green and Walter Hooper, *C. S. Lewis: A Biography* (New York: Harcourt Brace Jovanovich, 1974), p. 269.

happiness that passed me by in my twenties,"[9] he remarked to Nevill Coghill.

By autumn 1959 the cancer had returned. This time there was to be no miracle. Joy had long wanted to visit Greece. Lewis was very resistant to foreign travel, finding England and Ireland quite adequate for his wanderings, but in his desire to make Joy happy he agreed. Roger Green made the practical arrangements and accompanied them in April. Joy's pain was slowly increasing and she found walking harder than formerly, but the trip was a splendid and sometimes hilarious success. As reported by Lewis in a letter to me, Joy limped to the top of the Acropolis, climbed the hill to the lion gate at Mycenae, and roved the streets of Rhodes.

They returned to England. The cancer moved relentlessly. Surgery failed to stop it. On July 13, 1960, she died in the hospital. Two of the last things she said were, "You have made me happy," and "I am at peace with God."

Lewis never really recovered from the loss of Joy. When I next saw him in late 1961, he was

9. *C. S. Lewis: A Biography*, p. 270.

subdued and at loose ends. His own health had begun to fail. He had a combination of kidney and heart ailments; the attempt to alleviate one condition would aggravate the other. He had been a man of tremendous zest during most of his life, but toward the end I think he was ready for death.

Once before in his adult life Lewis had experienced the loss of someone to whom he was completely devoted, the writer, Charles Williams, in 1945. In the preface to *Essays Presented to Charles Williams*, Lewis said:[10]

This experience of loss (the greatest I have yet known) was wholly unlike what I should have expected. We now verified for ourselves what so many bereaved people have reported; the ubiquitous presence of a dead man, as if he had ceased to meet us in particular places in order to meet us everywhere. It is not in the least like a haunting. It is not in the least like the bitter-sweet experiences of memory. It is vital and bracing; it is even, however the word may be misunderstood and derided, exciting . . . . No event has so corroborated

10. (Grand Rapids: William B. Eerdmans, 1947, 1966.)

my faith in the next world as Williams did simply by dying. When the idea of death and the idea of Williams thus met in my mind, it was the idea of death that was changed.

The loss of Joy was of a different kind, and plunged Lewis into the very depths of despair. His religion, which had seemed so sturdily based, began to crumble. A meaningless or malevolent universe opened up at his feet.

In the first months after Joy's death Lewis kept a kind of journal written in occasional notebooks he found in his empty house. He eventually published it under the pseudonym of N. W. Clerk (a pun on the Old English for "I know not what scholar"). *A Grief Observed* was brought out just two years before his death. It was typical of Lewis's delicacy that it was published pseudonymously. In the midst of an agonized bereavement, Lewis records new insights that modify the neat certainties in his earlier books. It is implacably honest, and the tentative reassurances toward which it moves—the intuition of Joy's continued reality in another dimension of existence, the reality of

God's presence and love—are modestly stated, more suggested than stated. But as the book comes to an end, the reader finds himself sharing the first timid movement of Lewis back toward a world that makes sense. The night of loneliness and emptiness may plot further assaults, but the worst is, perhaps, over. Of the many books about bereavement I have read in recent years, this one is the most moving, with its absolute candor and determination to set down, day by day, the plain facts of agonizing experience.

After Lewis's death, his literary executors brought out additional books from scattered articles and manuscripts, bringing the total to more than fifty. Many of his works are clearly destined for a long life. Certainly he has left us a God's plenty. But one cannot help speculating. If he had been granted an additional ten years of good health, what might he have written? *Till We Have Faces, The Four Loves,* and *A Grief Observed* provide the clues. It was Joy that made them possible.

As I finish this little essay on Lewis and his Joy, I find my thoughts turning from literature to life. *A Grief Observed* points my memories to Jack and Joy, and their all too brief but gloriously meaningful marriage. Neither of them is a character straight out of a medieval courtly romance, but they learned from each other the mysteries of Friendship, Affection, Agape, and Eros at a depth that makes them kin to the great lovers found in literature and sometimes in life. *A Grief Observed* reveals the price paid for that knowledge. I do not think Lewis would have chosen to save the price and renounce the knowledge. In this most harrowing of his books, there is found also the radiance of a love that death itself could not dim. Lewis was indeed surprised by Joy—into his own self-knowledge and deepest fulfillment.

ABOUT C. S. LEWIS

C. S. Lewis was known to students at Cambridge University as a brilliant scholar and tutor, and to the world as an observer, author, and essayist of unusual distinction. His works include: *The Screwtape Letters, The Allegory of Love, Mere Christianity, The Chronicles of Narnia* (an acknowledged classic of fantasy), and his famous science fiction trilogy (*Out of the Silent Planet, Perelandra,* and *That Hideous Strength*). Born in Northern Ireland in 1898, he died at Oxford in November, 1963. C. S. Lewis had the rare gift of translating the concepts of Christianity into the language and the context of the everyday world.

ABOUT CHAD WALSH

Chad Walsh is a professor of English and writer-in-residence at Beloit College in Wisconsin. He is a poet who has published many books of poetry, edited several anthologies, and who has also written books on various aspects of religion. Like C. S. Lewis, he is a convert to the Christian faith. He is the author of a study of C. S. Lewis, entitled *C. S. Lewis: Apostle to the Sceptics.* Chad Walsh is currently at work on new poems and on a book dealing with the relationship between religion and the arts.